CREATING
Keepsakes
SCRAPBOOK MAGAZINE

You've got flair!
creative scrapbook techniques and more

This **fantastic book** is a compilation of *Creating Keepsakes'* best articles on finding your personal style and accessing your inner artist. You'll find **over 600 designs** and tips to **nudge your creativity** and teach you fun techniques for embellishing your **pages.** So turn the page and dive in — **it's time to play!**

time to let my inner artist run wild!

A TREASURY OF FAVORITES PRODUCED EXCLUSIVELY FOR LEISURE ARTS

Founding Editor	Lisa Bearnson
Editor-in-Chief	Brian Tippetts
Creative Editor	Britney Mellen
Editor-at-Large	Jana Lillie
Managing Editor	Brittany Beattie
Lifestyle Editor	Ali Edwards
Senior Editor	Vanessa Hoy
Senior Writer	Rachel Thomae
Associate Editor	Maurianne Dunn
Associate Writer	Lori Fairbanks
Project Manager	Lisa Ivey
Product Coordinator	Emily Magleby
Copy Editor	Kim Sandoval
Project Coordinator	Liesl Russell
Editorial Assistants	Joannie McBride, Fred Brewer
Contributing Editors	Brenda Arnall, Becky Higgins, Denise Pauley
Contributing Writers	Heather Jones, Jennifer McGuire
Art Director	Joleen Hughes
Senior Designer	Janice Barfuss
Production Designer	Matt Hill
Art Director, Special Projects	Erin Bayless
Senior Designer, Special Projects	Natalie Reich
Contributing Designers	Gaige Redd, ProDesign
Chief Executive Officer	David O'Neil

LEISURE ARTS
the art of everyday living

Vice President and Editor-in-Chief	Sandra Graham Case
Executive Director of Publications	Cheryl Nodine Gunnells
Senior Publications Director	Susan White Sullivan
Special Projects Director	Susan Frantz Wiles
Contributing Graphic Designer	Amy Vaughn
Director of Designer Relations	Debra Nettles
Senior Prepress Director	Mark Hawkins
Publishing Systems Administrator	Becky Riddle
Publishing Systems Assistants	Clint Hanson, John Rose, Keiji Yumoto
Vice President and Chief Operations Officer	Tom Siebenmorgen
Director of Corporate Planning and Development	Laticia Mull Dittrich
Vice President, Sales and Marketing	Pam Stebbins
Director of Sales and Services	Margaret Reinold
Vice President, Operations	Jim Dittrich
Comptroller, Operations	Rob Thieme
Retail Customer Service Manager	Stan Raynor
Print Production Manager	Fred F. Pruss

SUBSCRIPTIONS

To subscribe to Creating Keepsakes magazine or to change the address of your current subscription, call or write:

Phone: 888/247-5282
International: 760/745-2809
Fax: 760/745-7200

Subscriber Services
Creating Keepsakes
P.O. Box 469007
Escondido, CA 92046-9007

CORPORATE OFFICES

Creating Keepsakes is located at 14850 Heritagecrest Way, Bluffdale, UT 84065. Phone: 801/816-8300. Fax: 801/816-8301. Home page: www.creatingkeepsakes.com.

Library of Congress Control Number: 2007935184
Bearnson, Lisa
Creating Keepsakes
"A Leisure Arts Publication"

ISBN-13: 978-1-60140-527-2
ISBN-10: 1-60140-527-8

editor's
note

ONE OF THE THINGS I LOVE about looking through scrapbook albums is the variety of styles and how these styles show different personalities. There's something about adding your personal touch to a project that makes it *real*. After all, most of our scrapbooks record our personal and real experiences as well as those of our loved ones. This fantastic book is a compilation of *Creating Keepsakes'* best articles on finding your personal style and your inner artist.

Once you've found that personal style, spruce up those artistic skills by checking out articles such as "10 Sweet Chalk Tips" and "Oodles of Doodles." These articles give that little push we sometimes need to find ideas for using tried-and-true supplies.

So, pull up a chair, start finding your personal style and enhance your inner artist by reading through these great articles. You'll soon find yourself adding that creative personal touch on each of your scrapbook pages!

Have Fun,

Editor-in-Chief
Creating Keepsakes Magazine

101

THE FLANNIGAN CHARM

TOM

Flannigan Boys are absolutely adorable. My Father-in-Law, Tom, is no exception. And don't let appearances fool you, they aren't just handsome, they are super sweet and charming! I feel like a pretty lucky girl to be a part of the family! Kelsie 2005

contents

24

87

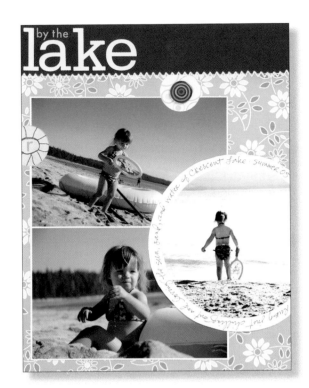

129

257

A CREATIVE NUDGE

ILLUSTRATION © CELESTE ROCKWOOD-JONES

Venture outside your comfort zone

I remember learning to play the guitar. At first, my fingers were so swollen they ached. I felt tempted to give up but resisted. "Give it more time," I thought. Soon my fingers started developing callouses—a good thing in guitar since they help cushion fingers. I played more chords and strummed along with tunes. Before long, my love of guitar was in full swing!

Ever feel uncomfortable about trying something new in scrapbooking? It's time for a creative nudge! Here's how five top designers took the challenge to step outside the box and try something that's a "first" for them. Follow their lead—it's always fun to surprise yourself and others.

BY LISA IVEY

the challenge

DARE TO DOODLE

Create a layout with doodling and no other embellishment.

This may seem easy—unless you're Jennifer McGuire and love to embellish. The assignment "forced" her to color outside the lines—literally—with doodling! This was a first for Jennifer. Because she felt a little hesitant about her hand-lettering, she traced letter stickers for better results.

the result

Says Jennifer, "I will definitely try this again. Doodling is so freeing—it made me feel like a kid again!"

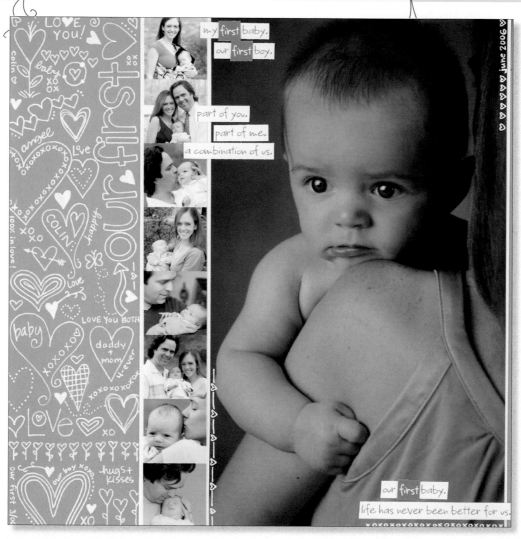

Our First Child by Jennifer McGuire. Photos by Angela Talentino, Essenza Studio. **Supplies** Cardstock: Bazzill Basics Paper; Letter stickers (for tracing title): Doodlebug Design; Pen: Stampin' Up!; Font: CK Footnote, downloaded from www.scrapnfonts.com.

"I don't really have a particular scrapbook style. One day I'll create something simple. The next, something more complicated. That's what I love about scrapbooking—there are no rules!"

—Jennifer McGuire

TIPS FOR THE FIRST-TIME DOODLER

Considering doodling for the first time? Jennifer recommends four practices:

1. Start with a pencil. Trace over your lines with a pen, then erase them.

2. Look at clip-art fonts and rubber stamps for inspiration when tracing.

3. Trace old letter stickers you won't use for a title.

4. Not sure you'll like the look? Try it first on a handmade card.

the challenge

DRESS IT UP!

Create a layout using patterned paper and embellishments.

Carrie—who typically takes the "cardstock and a pen" approach—found this task completely outside her comfort zone. Her clean, linear style doesn't usually include patterned paper (if so, only a tiny strip) or embellishments.

Here, Carrie not only used one pattern, but three. She added a few embellishments, then realized her layout wasn't balanced. To address this, she added a chipboard flower covered with brown dotted paper.

the result

Using patterned paper isn't as intimidating as Carrie thought it would be. She learned that she could incorporate new techniques yet stay true to her style.

Our First Home by Carrie Owens. **Supplies** *Cardstock, chipboard and brads:* Bazzill Basics Paper; *Patterned paper:* Chatterbox; *"1" wood accent:* Li'l Davis Designs; *Word-strip stickers:* 7gypsies; *Other:* Pen.

"Experimenting, especially in baby steps, is a great way to test new ideas and techniques. You just may surprise yourself. I know I did." —Carrie Owens

GO PHOTO-FREE
Create a layout without photos.

If you know anything about Candice Stringham, you'll understand why she calls herself a "photocentric" person. Her scrapbook pages are built around her photographs and usually have a classic, fun feel. The no-photo approach took her off-guard at first. Candice says, "I had to sit and think about it."

the result

Take away the photo and what do you have? Something amazing. The focus of Candice's layout is her journaling—a story about how she met her husband. She complemented this by adding elements with a "Shakespearean" feel. The pink patterned paper in the corner reminded Candice of "youthfulness" and meeting her husband in high school.

The First Time

The first time I saw you it was a warm fall day
I was the new girl simply trying to get
through the battlefield of
Timpview High School
You were the king of the theater department.

It was the weekend of the Cedar City
Shakespeare Competition and I was to compete
as Desdemona. You were Hamlet.

Two Tragedies

How could we have known ?

That two such sad roles could lead us to

Such complete

Happiness.

IDEA TO NOTE:
When scrapbooking without a photo, pull elements from the story and let those dictate your paper and embellishment choices.

The First Time by Candice Stringham. **Supplies** *Cardstock:* Bazzill Basics Paper; *Patterned paper:* BasicGrey (brown background), Scenic Route (pink background), Paper Source and Chatterbox; *Ink:* Distress Ink, Ranger Industries; *Ribbon:* May Arts; *Star gem:* Michaels; *Software:* Adobe Photoshop CS, Adobe Systems; *Brushes:* Rhonna Farrer, www.twopeasinabucket.com; *Fonts:* CK Roxy, "Fresh Fonts Vol. 2" CD; CK Letter Home, "Creative Clips & Fonts" CD, *Creating Keepsakes.*

the challenge

USE UP THOSE PHOTOS

Create a two-page layout using 10 or more photos!

Does using 10 photos on a layout intimidate you? How can you make all those photos feel cohesive? Take a peek at Jamie Waters' layout. Because she typically scraps one-photo layouts, she found it especially challenging to work on a larger canvas—and to envision where all her photos would be placed.

the result

Using more photos helped Jamie capture the charm and magnitude of her trip to Australia. Would she create another multi-photo layout? Yes!

AUS '05 *by Jamie Waters.* **Supplies** *Cardstock:* Bazzill Basics Paper; *Patterned paper and dimensional accents:* KI Memories; *Chipboard letters:* Heidi Swapp for Advantus; *Photo tabs:* SEI; *Letter stickers:* Gin-X, Imagination Project; *Number stickers:* Wordsworth; *Charm:* Carolee's Creations.

> *"Be willing to step out of your box to complete the challenge! You may find it's something you really enjoy."*
>
> —Jamie Waters

7 CHALLENGING FIRSTS!

Perhaps you've already mastered the 10-plus photo layout or the no-embellishment approach. Ready for new ideas? Here are seven additional "firsts" to try.

1. If you typically use a single color on your pages (monochromatic), spice things up with complementary colors instead.

2. Crop photos into circles instead of rectangles.

3. Instead of cropping your photos, use all 4" x 6" photos on your page.

4. Try your hand at a digital layout instead of a traditional page.

5. If you always handwrite your journaling, print your journaling using the computer.

6. Feeling stuck in your journaling style? Forego handwritten journaling and use stickers or hand-cut letters instead.

7. For die-hard 12" x 12" scrappers, go 8½" x 11", 8" x 8" or make a mini album.

FILL IT UP

Create a layout that fills the entire page and uses multiple photos.

With a graphic design background, Laura Kurz prefers a simple, straight-line approach to scrapbooking. She calls herself a "self-proclaimed lover of white space" and it's easy to see why. Her layouts typically have a very large border around the edge.

Filling a page was quite a challenge. To meet the challenge, Laura conceptualized her page as eight separate blocks, rather than one large page.

the result

Creating a layout with little white space made it easier for Laura to do a multi-photo layout—something she struggles with. She mixed and matched several products to see which would complement each other.

IDEA TO NOTE: Laura intentionally overlapped the rub-ons (stars, scroll and words) onto the brown cardstock to make the "white space" around the eight rectangles less obvious. ❤

Learning *by Laura Kurz.* **Supplies** *Cardstock:* My Mind's Eye; *Patterned paper:* Scenic Route (circles) and Making Memories (polka dot, orange floral and blue floral); *Rub-ons:* American Crafts ("learning"), Chatterbox (scrolls), Heidi Swapp for Advantus (stars) and Making Memories; *Stamps:* FontWerks; *Ink:* Stampin' Up!; *Staples:* Making Memories.

Relax and Play

Come pipe, etch and dye with me—it's easy!

Every so often I end up with a few spare hours. I consider what I "should" do—you know, clean my house, shop for groceries or weed the garden. Then I put those thoughts aside and focus on something more fun—like racing to my studio to play with paint and other mediums. I can't help it!

During these short sessions, I like to experiment with techniques and make accents for future projects. I may finish a scrapbook page or card . . . or not. Mostly I just relax and enjoy discovering fresh takes like the four shared here. They're looks you won't find other places, and they're super-easy to duplicate. Here's how!

by Helen Williams

2"diameter on Maya Road tin

Make a darling mini card!

thanks

Pipe a Few Flowers

Create cute flowers (or stars, hearts, leaves and other outlines) from texture pastes. They're fun, fresh, fairly sturdy and *you* control the size, color and shape. To create this look:

❶ With a palette knife, mix together texture paste and paint in a 3:1 ratio.

❷ Use scissors to snip a small hole in the corner of a Ziploc bag. Scoop paste into the bag and push it toward the hole.

❸ Pipe the flowers onto baking paper with a smooth, flowing motion. Position the bag tip slightly above the paper for greater control.

silly | moody | sweet | Prima donna

loving

nine :-)

Erin

Feb. '06 | 8

Erin *by Helen Williams.* **Supplies** *Texture paste and dimensional paint:* Jo Sonja's; *Pen:* Tough Ball, Marvy Uchida.

④ Let the flowers dry for several hours. When they're dry, slide the edge of a palette knife gently under each flower to lift it from the baking paper.

⑤ Attach each flower to your project with liquid adhesive. Store any extras for use as quick custom accents.

Helen's Tips

- Expect to "fudge" a few flowers at first. Practice makes perfect! While you're at it, create leaves, scrolls and other shapes as well.

- Determine how thick your flower will be by the size of the hole in the piping bag.

- For the smoothest results, work slightly above the paper surface and avoid dragging the bag tip.

- Mess up? Before the paste starts to set, simply scoop it up and put it back in the piping bag.

- Use scissors to cut rough or overhanging edges off your flower once it's dry.

Hand-Dip Fabric the Ziploc Way

Love the look of dyed fabric and want to use it on a scrapbook page? Achieve dramatic results fast—and avoid messy cleanup—with the help of a simple Ziploc bag. Here's how:

kicking back on the veranda. Feb. 2006

Summer *by Helen Williams.* **Supplies** *Texture paste and paint:* Jo Sonja's; *Dye:* Dye Na Flow, Jacquard Products; *Pen:* Tough Ball, Marvy Uchida; *Flowers:* Bumblebee Crafts (small) and unknown (large); *Letter stickers:* American Crafts; *Chipboard circle:* Collections; *Large brad:* Bazzill Basics Paper.

① Place fabric inside a Ziploc bag.

② Spritz with water so the fabric is damp but not saturated.

③ Using 2–3 colors (more of the lightest and less of the darker), drip the dye onto the fabric.

3 Steps

TO A BEAUTIFUL BACKGROUND

Want to create a background like that on my "Summer" page? Simply:

1. Apply a thick layer of texture paste to medium-weight cardboard, as described in Step 1 on page 14.

2. Lay pieces of dyed fabric over the wet paste.

3. Blend the pieces into the background with a palette knife. Let dry thoroughly.

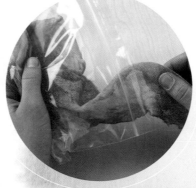

4. Close the bag and squeeze the fabric so the dye is distributed throughout it. Avoid overmixing—you don't want a solid dye color.

5. Remove the fabric to check on the progress. (Use tweezers or disposable gloves if you're worried about staining your fingers.) If you find large areas of undyed fabric, continue working. If not, remove the fabric and lay it out to dry.

Helen's Tips

- Use natural fabrics (like cotton or the cheesecloth here). They take up dye readily, ensuring more vibrant results.

- To speed up drying time, dry the fabric with a hair dryer, in a clothes dryer (I've not had a problem with staining) or with a carefully applied heat gun.

Etch a Design

Etching a design into texture paste creates a cool, artistic background. Paint it for a highlighted effect as shown here, or leave it plain for a textural, minimalist effect. To duplicate this look:

① Create a base with a medium-weight piece of cardboard (approximately four times the thickness of cardstock). Use a palette knife to "butter" a thick layer of texture paste over the entire surface. Pull the paste in different directions to create a random, uneven texture.

② While the paste is still wet, use the tip of a stylus, or skewer, to etch a design into the paste. Go over any lines as needed to create a strong impression. Clean the tip of the etching tool regularly to avoid paste buildup.

③ Add texture to the flower center by pouncing the tip of the palette knife into the paste. Let the paste dry thoroughly (for several hours or overnight, depending on your climate).

playing with tabby . games . fun .

holidays . pink .

the Best Things

purple . chickens . birthdays . christmas . swimming

The Best Things by *Helen Williams*. **Supplies** *Texture paste and paint:* Jo Sonja's; *Rub-ons:* Making Memories; *Pen:* Tough Ball, Marvy Uchida.

④ Paint over your design with watered-down acrylic paint.

⑤ Use darker, more vibrant paint (achieved by adding less water) in the etched lines of the design for greater detail.

Helen's Tips

- Protect your work surface with a sheet of plastic or paper.

- Etch the design into the texture paste before it begins to set, generally within 20–30 minutes.

- Mess up while etching? Smooth the area over with a palette knife and continue.

Mask and Embellish

As we wrap up a few fun looks with dimension and paint, I couldn't resist showing the eye-catching looks you can create with simple "mask and embellish" steps. For a closer view (and step-by-step instructions), see the next page.

The best thing about staying at Mandeni...the parrots! They would fly in every day to be handfed - right on our doorstep!! At any given time we would have King Parrots, Crimson Rosellas & Rainbow Lorikeets (pictured) jockeying for a feeding position. So cool! We loved it!!

Mandeni *by Helen Williams.* **Supplies** *Stamps:* Making Memories; *Dimensional paint for highlighting designs:* Adirondack, Ranger Industries; *Acrylic paint for stamping flowers:* Jo Sonja's; *Font:* 2Peas Stained Glass, downloaded from *www.twopeasinabucket.com*.

Dazzle with dots and lines!

Where to Find What You'll Need

Love the products used to create these scrapbook pages? Visit your local art or scrapbook store, or visit the websites below.

- Jo Sonja's (*www.josonja.com*)
- Jacquard Products (*www.jacquardproducts.com*)

- American Crafts (*www.americancrafts.com*)
- Bazzill Basics Paper (*www.bazzillbasics.com*)
- Bumblebee Crafts (*www.bumblebeecrafts.com.au*)
- Collections (e-mail *collections@westnet.com.au*)
- Making Memories (*www.makingmemories.com*)
- Marvy Uchida (*www.uchida.com*)
- Maya Road (*www.mayaroad.com*)
- Ranger Industries (*www.rangerink.com*)

① Create one or more masks. Stamp onto scrap paper the foreground images that will need to be protected in the final design. Cut out as accurately as possible.

② Stamp the foreground images of the design onto your layout..

③ Position the "mask" created in Step 1 over the corresponding area of the design that you wish to protect while stamping your background images.

④ Stamp the background images of the design. Remove masks.

⑤ Embellish the stamped designs with dimensional paint.

Helen's Tips

- Let each layer of stamped images dry before stamping any overlapping images.

- Using dimensional paint? Get the "flow" going on a scrap of paper first to avoid air bubbles or blobs when the paint first comes out.

- Work the dimensional paint onto the flowers in stages, stopping and moving the paper around as you draw to avoid smearing the paint. ♥

Artistic Journaling

I'M AN AVID DOODLER. You'll find hearts on my phone book and happy faces on my to-do lists. If you're a doodler as well, you've probably included a few of your favorite images in your scrapbook. If you're not, it's easier than you think to create simple illustrations for your pages—images that will add flair to your journaling and catch everyone's eye.

It's time to find your inner artist. Grab a pencil, an eraser and some pens, then try out this creative journaling technique yourself!

Decorate a can label with a recipe for a festive holiday gift. Label by Danielle Donaldson. **Supplies** *Cardstock:* Prism Papers and Bazzill Basics Paper; *Patterned paper:* KI Memories and Rusty Pickle; *Ink:* Ranger Industries; *Pens:* American Crafts (black) and Stampin' Up! (colors). Tag by Danielle Donaldson. **Supplies** *Cardstock:* Bazzill Basics Paper; *Patterned paper:* KI Memories; *Brads:* Making Memories; *Pens:* EK Success and Stampin' Up!; *Leaf punch:* EK Success; *Other:* Ribbon and twill.

DANIELLE DONALDSON
Danielle has always enjoyed the arts, earning her bachelor's degree in graphic design. She indulges in her artistic roots by combining drawing and painting with scrapbooking. A California native, Danielle lives in the Sacramento area with her husband, Scott, and two children, Lauren and Clay.

artful words

1 Select a simple image. Sketch in pencil on your cardstock. *Note:* You can trace a shape from a template or around a punched shape for a simpler option.

Outline image with a fine-tip black pen. Add a decorative border around image with black pen. Let the ink dry, then erase pencil lines with a white vinyl eraser.

2 Write your text using different widths of pen tips, such as the 0.1 mm and 0.5 mm tips in this sample. Use various sizes and styles of handwriting to nest words together and create visual interest.

3 Color image and border with brush-tip pens—experiment with just three colors when you start using this technique. Add shadows to the illustration as well.

4 Complete the project by tracing your lettering with the same brush-tip pens you used to color your image and border. Use assorted pen tips to emphasize words differently.

helpful hints

- Use pale, translucent pen colors to let your lettering show through more clearly.

- Look through children's books, labels and greeting cards for simple images to copy.

- Practice makes perfect! As you're learning, spend the time to draw your object and words in pencil first.

- Pull out your stash of lettering templates and trace your letters lightly with pencil. Remove the template and "freehand" the letters with a fine-tip pen, then use brush-tip pens to loosely outline the letters for a hand-drawn effect.

- When drawing your objects, think of each as a group of simple shapes, such as triangles, circles and rectangles.

- Instead of adding images to your journaling, make them a part of it. How? Replace simple words like "boy," "puppy," "milk" or "cookies" with an image representing the word (this technique is called a rebus).

- Watercolor pencils can be used instead of markers. ❤

Use colored fibers and ribbon that match your lettering to create a coordinated look on your layout. *Page by Danielle Donaldson.* **Supplies** *Cardstock:* Bazzill Basics Paper; *Patterned paper:* Junkitz; *Brads:* Making Memories; *Paw punch:* McGill; *Ink:* Ranger Industries; *Pens:* American Crafts (black) and Stampin' Up! (colors); *Other:* Ribbon and fibers.

capture life.
create art.

Edwards '06

let's play

by ALI EDWARDS

Sometimes I think we take this hobby *way* too seriously. Sometimes I think we need to enjoy the process more. Embrace the imperfection inherent in creating. Take a break from overthinking everything. Here, take a look at a few ways you can bring more play into your scrapbooking process. >

One of my main scrapbooking mottos is:

it is okay.

- **It is okay** to play.
- **It is okay** to make mistakes (*this is how we learn and grow*).
- **It is okay** to not scrapbook chronologically.
- **It is okay** to mix patterned papers that don't match exactly.
- **It is okay** to do whatever feels best to you.
- **It is okay** to experiment.

Focusing on play has helped me maintain my love of scrapbooking. Trying new things and experimenting and evolving— these are essential for creative growth. It's way too easy to get stuck in the same-old, same-old. Are you ready? Let's play!

WAYS TO PLAY: THE BASICS

❶ Forget about whatever rules you think exist. Rules can be valuable, but they can also be stifling. Just for today, take a break from your personal scrapbooking rules. Do something different.

❷ Give yourself permission to play today like a child, if only for one day, without fear of making a mistake, without fear of judgment. Without fear that whatever you're creating is "right" or "wrong." There is no right or wrong in scrapbooking. What is so very right is that you are taking the time to do it at all.

❸ Keep it simple. Don't think that play means complicated art. The idea here is simply to free yourself to try something new. Start with just one little bit of your layout.

R & S *by Ali Edwards.*
Supplies *Cardstock:* Bazzill Basics Paper; *Patterned paper:* American Crafts, Creative Imaginations, Mustard Moon and Scenic Route; *Circle cutter:* Creative Memories; *Circle punches:* Marvy Uchida and Punch Bunch; *Circle tags:* SEI; *Circle initials:* Heidi Swapp for Advantus; *Circle stickers:* 7gypsies, Creative Imaginations and Pebbles Inc.; *Ink:* Stampin' Up!.

Ali's notes

PLAY WITH SIZE AND SHAPE

> The key to playing with shapes is to vary the size, texture and pattern. This keeps things interesting and fun.

> I hope you noticed that using blurry photos is fine. It is okay, my friends. It is okay.

today you found **SLEEP** in our bed

Today *by Ali Edwards.* **Supplies** *Patterned papers:* KI Memories and Danny O, K&Company; *Word stickers:* K&Company; *Rub-ons:* Autumn Leaves (letters) and KI Memories (circle); *Stamps:* Paper Source; *Ink:* Ranger Industries, Stampin' Up! and Tsukineko; *Embossing powder:* Ranger Industries,; *Mask:* Heidi Swapp for Advantus; *Book tape:* 7gypsies; *Ribbon:* May Arts; *Pen:* American Crafts; *Font:* Avenir, Adobe Systems; *Other:* Velcro, and a board book from a monthly kit at *www.self-addressed.com.*

Ali's notes

**PLAY WITH SOMETHING TOTALLY
NEW FOR YOU**

> This is one of my favorite recent projects. I love that I was able to try something new to me (especially embossing over the mask) and that it didn't have to become a super-complicated endeavor. I simply covered each page in the board book with a piece of patterned paper, used one stamp to unify each page, and added a bit of journaling to personalize the story.

❶ Add Velcro to ribbon to create a closure.

❷ Emboss something. Here, I embossed over a mask. Lay the mask over the board book and press firmly. Apply embossing ink over the mask. Add embossing powder and cook it with a heat gun.

❸ Add type directly onto a photo. Use rub-ons, stickers or a photo-editing program such as Adobe Photoshop Elements.

❹ Pretend you're a fabulous book author and use photos and scrapbooking supplies to tell a story from your life.

FRONT

BACK

ENCLOSURE

NICS TIME TOGETHER GOOD BOOKS CARTWHEELS

OBJECTS MAY BE LARGER THAN THEY APPEAR

A TRUE STORY
PROFILE

THE FAITH THAT THE SUN WILL RISE TOMORROW AND THAT THIS TOO WILL PASS   KIND WORDS   MUSIC   A WAGGING TAI

REFUGE IN A STORM   COZY   SAFE HAVEN   RETREAT

❋ BE
OrGANic

PROOF

WHO WHAT WHEN WHERE HOW DA   DATES IF ONLY E

I think that scrapbooking makes me love coffee even more. Wakes me up + keeps me up to meet deadlines (or catch up ☺). I love it SUPER HOT. Black. **NO SUBSTITUTIONS** Just plain + hot... totally keeps me happy.

I do the most crazy stuff because of this hobby. Like photos of my coffee cups (not just one photo — but lots). And photos of myself... Now this is good, but it is still a bit wacky... + that fits ☺.

notes
notes
no note
notes
notes
notes

A True Story by Ali Edwards. **Supplies:** *Textured cardstock:* Bazzill Basics Paper; *Patterned paper:* American Crafts; *Sticky notes:* Heidi Swapp for Advantus; *Circle accent:* 7gypsies; *Circle rub-on:* BasicGrey; *Rub-on phrases:* 7gypsies.

play |plā| |pleɪ| |ple| • verb
1 engage in activity for enjoyment
and recreation rather than a
serious or practical purpose.

Ali's notes

PLAY WITH PHOTOGRAPHY

> Take photos of yourself and scrap them. Stand in front of a window in your home and hold your camera out in front of your face and click away. Take lots of photos. And then take some more. The more you take, the more likely it will be that you'll take one you enjoy, one that captures you in the moment.

Happy by Ali Edwards. **Supplies** *Cardstock:* Bazzill Basics Paper; *Patterned paper and pen:* American Crafts; *"S" tab:* Die Cuts With a View; *Letter stickers:* Heidi Swapp for Advantus.

Ali's notes

PLAY WITH PHOTOS

> Pull out some of your photos that are totally imperfect. I tend to say I LOVE YOU to photos that really capture the essence of life. Something about them makes me perfectly happy.

Play is super-important in your own development as a creative individual. Here are some other ideas to help you play:

- Read a cool book, like *52 Projects: Random Acts of Everyday Creativity* by Jeffrey Yamaguchi (you can find out more online at *www.52projects.com*).

- Listen to music that makes it impossible not to play. Right now I'm all about Johnny Cash and June Carter Cash.

- Invite friends over to scrap. Make play the focus of the night. *Make a rule that you all have to try something new.* In fact, have each person come with something to teach the rest of the group. ❤

Roses *by Sharon Laakkonen.* **Supplies** *Cardstock:* Bazzill Basics Paper; *Patterned paper:* me & my BIG ideas; *Chipboard letters:* Imagination Project; *Stamp:* Fontwerks; *Pen:* Sharpie, Sanford; *Flowers:* Doodlebug Design; *Ink:* Ranger Industries; *Digital brush:* Spaceraven.net.

Fancy Frames

I've discovered a quick and easy way to create frames, decorated photo corners, titles and photo edges. To make these hand-drawn doodles, stamp a curvy design with light-colored ink. Then trace over the stamped image with a pen. (Some of the ink may show through—this just adds a sense of dimension!)

Try stamping on chipboard letters to give them a whole new look. The frames on the photo continue the doodled look—they were added in Adobe Photoshop, then printed out.

—*Sharon Laakkonen, Superior, WI* ❤

Oodles of Doodles

Be creative and carefree

We all doodle—on pads of paper when we're on the phone, in the margins of notebooks, in newspapers as we read. And now doodling has become a popular look in scrapbooking, too! Forget the days of doodling simply to pass the time. Doodling can help you add a fresh look to your scrapbooking style.

Simply grab your pencil or pen and join in the fun! Doodling will help you develop creativity and express "you" on any layout.

by jennifer purdie

Family *by Danielle Thompson.* **Supplies** *Cardstock:* Bazzill Basics Paper; *Rub-ons:* 7gypsies, Autumn Leaves, Provo Craft and Heidi Swapp for Advantus; *Puff flower, button and epoxy circle sticker:* Autumn Leaves; *Sequins:* Westrim Crafts; *Foam flower:* Michaels; *Embroidery floss:* DMC; *Wooden flower:* Li'l Davis Designs; *Ink:* Marvy Matchables, Marvy Uchida; VersaColor, Tsukineko; *White pen:* Uni-ball Signo, Sanford; *Colored pens:* Sakura and EK Success.

Draw easy shapes as a simple solution for creating a doodled look without a lot of practice. Try this idea from Danielle Thompson! On this page, she doodled simple flower shapes on cardstock, then cut them out and inked them.

laughter
is an
instant
vacation

VACATION

folsom
Lake
lauren and clay
summer '05

Vacation *by Danielle Donaldson.* **Supplies** *Patterned paper and stickers:* Memories Complete; *Pens and corner rounder:* EK Success; *Ink:* Stampin' Up!; *Ribbon:* May Arts.

Create a "signature doodle." Find something that's easy for you to doodle and make it your "thing." If you're not comfortable drawing several doodles or a new doodle on every page, a signature doodle lets you perfect one look, then add it to your layout for a special touch without a lot of stress. Danielle's signature doodle is a series of swirls that connect different parts of her layout.

★ ★ ★ ★ ★ ★ ★ ★ ★ ★ ★ ★ ★ ★ ★ ★ ★ ★

outside—mark them, they are most useful players, out from among the chargers, and away with it across the dodgers—they seize on the

Photo taken – July 2005
Then the boys who are bending and watching on the

to the opposite goal. They seldom go into the scrum-

BROT
HERS

i wondered so much about the type of relationship the two of you would have when i was pregnant with Christian. Would you fight? Would you defend each other? Would you love one another—unconditionally? Would you share the same interests? Would you lean on one another? Truth is, it's been a little bit of all the above. Each day i see a different side or an evolution of the relationship. Much like any relationship. It has been such a joy to witness it.

Brothers *by Jenni Bowlin.* **Supplies** *Patterned paper:* Scrapworks; *Rubberstamp letters:* Stampin' Up!; *Star stamps:* Vintage; *Rub-ons and chipboard heart:* Heidi Swapp for Advantus; *Epoxy letters:* Li'l Davis Designs; *Ribbon:* C.M. Offray & Son; *Glitter:* Art Institute.

Make guides with your rubber-stamped images, like the stars in Jenny's layout, for handwritten journaling (so a blank background won't seem so overwhelming). Or, add handwritten boxes, circles and more around rubber-stamped letters in a title and fill them in with colored pencils.

Look Deeper *by Elsie Flannigan.* **Supplies** *Textured cardstock:* Bazzill Basics Paper; *Patterned paper:* KI Memories; *Letter stickers and flower:* Heidi Swapp for Advantus; *Ribbon:* May Arts and C.M. Offray & Son; *Pen:* American Crafts.

Doodle directly on a photo—be brave! You can create a border, a fun accent or cute word art! Get creative—you can journal on more than just the background.

Tip: When writing on photos, remember to use acid-free, permanent markers and pens. Gel pens come in a variety of colors and work great for journaling and outlining letters.

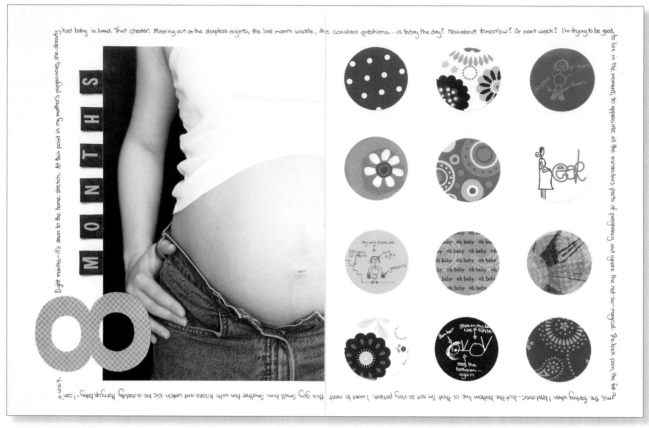

8 Months *by Traci Turchin.* **Supplies** *Patterned paper:* Chatterbox, SEI, KI Memories, BasicGrey, Anna Griffin and foof-a-La, Autumn Leaves; *Rubber stamps:* A Muse Artstamps; *Ink:* ColorBox, Clearsnap; *Rub-ons:* KI Memories; *Tabs:* Scrapworks; *Software:* Adobe Photoshop CS, Adobe Systems.

Scan your doodles and turn them into Photoshop brushes. To do this, simply scan in your doodle and open up the image in Photoshop. In the edit menu, click on "define brush preset" and *voila*, an instant Photoshop brush! You can then manipulate your doodle to be any size or color. Or, layer it on top of a photo before printing without worrying about mistakes.

Learn to Love It!

Eager to learn but a bit hesitant? Here are a few doodling tips to help:

- Doodle time is anytime. Carry scratch paper with you. Who knows? You might come up with the perfect idea while watching TV or listening to the radio.

- Doodle simply for practice. It will help you relax *and* develop your creativity.

- Like other techniques, doodling requires practice. Doodle often!

- Instead of doodling directly on your page, doodle on an accent block that can be added later. If your doodle doesn't turn out as hoped, you can redo the block without redoing the entire background of your page.

- Enjoy that you're leaving a record of your handwriting for future generations to see. That's rare with all the e-mail nowadays! ♥

Become a Doodling Diva!

BY SUZANNE QUILLEN

Doodling is not a new trend, but it has never been hotter than it is right now. Not only does it add whimsy and flair to your scrapbook pages, but it's fun to do! There are no wrong or right ways to doodling, so have some fun and make it yours. All you really need are a good fine-tip pen, a pencil, eraser and creativity to go from drab to fab!

In this tutorial, you will learn the basic swirl, the loopy swirl and extensions. At that point, you'll have a good understanding of how to create swirls that are all your own!

BASIC SWIRL

Step 1: Use your pencil to make a nice flowing swirl.

Step 2: Trace over your pencil marking with your fine-tip pen and then add your "depth lines."

Step 3: Fill in your depth-line spaces with your pen.

LOOPY SWIRL

Step 1: Use your pencil to make a nice flowing swirl. Note that the difference between the basic swirl is that we have now added a small loop. The loop should be on the opposite side of the swirl. In the example, you will see my loop goes up, and my swirl goes down.

Step 2: Trace over your pencil marking with the pen and add depth lines. I like adding my depth lines at the tail (where you start your swirl), over the loop and around the crown of the swirl.

Step 3: Fill in depth-line spaces with your pen.

EXTENSIONS

Extensions are a combination of basic swirls and loopy swirls connected together to create one artistic accent. Use the steps above to create your own! ♥

ultra-creative lettering

Boost your handwriting with these doable tips!

As a first grader, my favorite part of the school day was practicing my writing. It looked atrocious (hey, I was just seven!), but I loved the feel of the PENCIL and dragging it ever so carefully to print my letters. Soon I was experimenting with cursive, and eventually I developed a style that was all my own.

Years later, I still love the fresh, personal touch a person's creative lettering can add to a project. Still hoping to develop a more distinctive style myself, I asked five creative lettering experts to share samples and their favorite techniques. I was amazed at the results! Check out these women's lettering advice, then create a cool masterpiece of your own. You might even SCORE some extra credit!

by LISA IVEY

Add Your Own Touches

With *creative* lettering, your writing doesn't have to be perfect! At least that's how Sherelle Christensen feels about her fun and whimsical style. She takes a "go with the flow, mix it up" approach, using both *cursive* and *print* and randomly mixing *uppercase* and *lowercase* letters (see her layout).

Sherelle took her lettering up a notch by *bolding* and *enlarging* certain key words. She then used pink and green colored pencils to accentuate them.

Sisters *by Sherelle Christensen.* **Supplies** *Cardstock:* Making Memories; *Patterned paper and tags:* Melissa Frances; *"S":* foof-a-La, Autumn Leaves; *Ribbon and rickrack:* May Arts; *Other:* Button and colored pencils.

A black Pilot pen (V-Ball .05) is perfect for lettering because it doesn't "bleed."

SHERELLE'S ADVICE

"I always try to include my handwriting somewhere on my pages . . . it makes them seem much more personal."

Ready for more? Although Danielle used the same techniques as Sherelle, she went one step further by adding *letter stickers.* Not only do these help the letters stand out, they make each word its own piece of art.

Danielle also added a thin, black line around the stickers and a touch of color (from the *brush tip of a marker*) for emphasis. See what you can do with these fun, easy techniques!

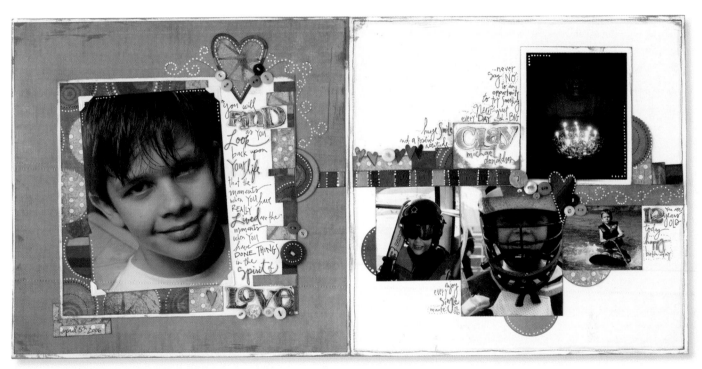

Spirit of Love *by Danielle Donaldson.* **Supplies** *Patterned paper:* Fancy Pants Designs and BasicGrey; *Stickers:* BasicGrey; *Paint pen:* Delta Creative; *Punch:* EK Success; *Pens:* EK Success and Stampin' Up!; *Ink:* Ranger Industries; *Other:* Buttons and photo corners.

"Handwriting is a little about who you are, wrapped up in lines and curves and letter spacing."
—ANNIE WHEATCRAFT, *friend of Danielle*

Bring Out the Craft Knife

Want a truly unique lettering style? *Hand-cut* your letters as Carrie did. Along with her clean and simple style, the tall ascenders and descenders (shown on the "Smiles" title) add a *special* touch.

gotta love ice cream

smiles

Why is it that kids don't care if their face is so very dirty with ice cream? How do they not know that their fingers are slimy? Why do they grin and grin at the sight of a pink spoon? How can one small sweet scoop send them into orbit?

How is it that grown ups have lost this ability to find joy in a polka dot cup?

summer '05

Ice Cream Smiles *by Carrie Owens.* **Supplies** *Cardstock:* Prism Papers and Bazzill Basics Paper; *Patterned paper:* Mustard Moon; *Rub-on stitches:* Die Cuts With a View.

Whether you're a beginner or an expert at creative lettering, consider these helpful hints:

7

TIPS TO SAVE YOU TIME & TROUBLE

1

Keep a notebook with you at all times. You can write down ideas while you're waiting in line at the grocery store!

2

Write your letters in pencil first (in case you mess up). Once you've mastered the technique, use pen.

3

Let go of any reservations. There's not a "wrong" way to letter creatively!

4

When choosing a lettering style, consider the type of mood you want to create on your layout.

EASY STEPS TO HAND-CUT LETTERING

 Using a ruler and a pencil, sketch your letters onto a piece of cardstock.

 Use a sharp craft knife and glass mat (or cardboard) to cut out the inside of the letters first. Be sure to turn your page, not the knife, for smooth curves.

Once the letters are adhered to your layout, carefully erase any stray pencil marks.

 Think of each word as its own piece of art.

 Use a variety of pen tips, plus a combination of print/cursive and upper-case/lowercase letters as appropriate. You'll create visual interest (and hide a few mistakes if needed).

 Practice, practice, practice. Your lettering will reflect it.

CK Fonts Online!

Look through this article again, and you'll notice that many of these techniques can be added to journaling printed with fonts! Ready to give it a try? You'll find numerous CK fonts that are sure to inspire at *www.scrapnfonts.com!*

EXTRA CREDIT

Want to add *texture* and dimension to your hand-cut letters? Try Elsie's fun, hip technique. She *matted* her hand-cut words on lime cardstock, then trimmed around the edges. To help the letters "pop" visually, Elsie used a white pen to draw multiple "outlines" inside each letter. She highlighted each word by *doodling* along the outside edge.

Best Friends *by Elsie Flannigan.* **Supplies** *Cardstock:* Bazzill Basics Paper; *Patterned paper:* BasicGrey; *Ribbon and rickrack:* Chatterbox and May Arts; *Epoxy accent:* KI Memories and Autumn Leaves; *Photo tape:* Heidi Swapp for Advantus; *White pen:* Uni-ball Signo, Sanford; *Other:* Buttons.

ELSIE'S ADVICE

"Don't be afraid to be 'messy.' It can make your pages unique and special!"

Creatively Embellish with Ease

Do you cringe at the sight of your handwriting? If you're not confident showing it off, this technique is for you. Simply *mask* the letters with an embellishment, such as flowers. Here, Kim formed an "a" monogram from *flowers,* then secured it with brads.

I don't know how it all started but when Alayna is bored with me taking pictures of her, she threatens to kiss me. Of course this is a good thing but it doesn't do me any good to have (kissy face) pictures either. So this is my cue to stop with the pictures. Of course until ne time. . .shhhhh

A Kiss *by Kim Hughes.* **Supplies** *Cardstock:* Bazzill Basics Paper; *Patterned paper:* CherryArte; *Ink:* Stampin' Up!; *Ribbon:* Prima and A.C. Moore; *Brads:* Creative Impressions; *Flowers and chipboard letters:* Prima; *Acrylic paint:* Plaid Enterprises; *Font:* 2Peas Roxie, downloaded from *www.twopeasinabucket.com.*

Other Ideas

What if using flowers to mask your lettering isn't for you? Try these other cool ways to accentuate them:

- Sew a straight or zigzag stitch along the letters.
- Add small items like brads, eyelets, staples, safety pins, beads or rhinestones.
- Apply small rub-on words.
- Add tied ribbon or bows.
- Adhere punched shapes.
- Glue or sew on buttons.

ADD PIZZAZZ WITH 7 MORE TECHNIQUES

Now that you've mastered the three previous handwriting assignments, you're no doubt ready for more. Check out these seven cool techniques from Danielle Donaldson!

Combine your hand-lettering with stamps and computer journaling.

Create a flower stem out of your hand-lettering. Place your words on a curve for a funky touch!

Break up chunky text into smaller blocks to give your lettering "breathing room." Create visual interest by making a key word bigger in each block and adding color.

Add flair by breaking up lines of text with scraps of ribbon or rickrack.

Use handwritten journaling to create a design within your design. Group your lettering within a photo to create a frame around people or objects.

Spice up hand-cut lettering with small blocks of color.

Replace labels on crayons with a personalized handwritten message. Get creative with other supplies around your home as well! ♥

ADDICTED To TYPE

Channel your passion for lettering

HI MY NAME IS BRENDA, AND I'M ADDICTED TO TYPE.

I confess—I'm fixated on fonts, in love with letter stickers, rabid about rub-ons and avid about alphabet stamps. Whether these letterforms are tiny or super-sized, plain or fancy, I love them all, and I'll bet you feel the same way.

Letterforms are an integral part of page design. Their size, style and weight express theme and mood just as much as other decorative elements on the page. They help tell the story.

While our addiction to letterforms may never be cured, we can manage their use to achieve better page design. Here's the first step to recovery: three layouts that illustrate font do's and don'ts in titles and journaling. See you at the next meeting!

by BRENDA ARNALL

SET THE
mood

Use a font that fits the mood of your layout. If your layout is serious or emotional, choose a font that conveys the same feeling. If your layout is fun, choose a playful, funky font. Just make sure it's readable!

FONT IN VERSION A

- Doesn't match mood of layout.
- Hard to read in all caps with tight line spacing.

Version A

www.lovekayla.com *by Brenda Arnall.* **Supplies** *Cardstock:* Bazzill Basics Paper; *Patterned paper:* Karen Foster Design (white dots) and KI Memories; *Pens:* Pigma Micron, Sakura; *Ribbon:* May Arts; *Envelope:* Brenda's own design; *Fonts:* Funky Fun (Version A) and Gill Sans MT (Version B), downloaded from the Internet; CK Fraternity (Version C), "Creative Clips & Fonts" CD, *Creating Keepsakes; Other:* Buttons and cord

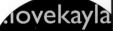

FONT IN VERSION B

- Clean lines.
- Easy to read with upper- and lowercase letters and more line spacing.

Idea to note: To create the title, Brenda made a text box, changed the font color to pink and the fill to black, then output the title on photo paper.

www.lovekayla.com

"Hi, Grandma!" I can almost hear the lilt of her voice as I read the words. Kayla has learned to e-mail, and we have a new way to stay in touch. Each message isn't more than a couple of sentences but it brings a smile to my face. She writes just like she talks, a snapshot in words of her sunny personality and her life at the moment. The misspellings, homonyms and typing errors only add to the charm. Her playroom now contains her own computer and desk, complete with a handmade sign declaring the area "Kayla's Office." And I chuckle to myself at all of the stuffed animals and toys that inhabit her "office." Sentimental grandmother that I am, I just had to save these early e-mails from my favorite girl, all sweetly signed "Love, Kayla."
December 2004

Version C

Version B

www.lovekayla.com

"Hi, Grandma!" I can almost hear the lilt of her voice as I read the words. Kayla has learned to e-mail, and we have a new way to stay in touch. Each message isn't more than a couple of sentences but it brings a smile to my face. She writes just like she talks, a snapshot in words of her sunny personality and her life at the moment. The misspellings, homonyms and typing errors only add to the charm. Her playroom now contains her own computer and desk, complete with a handmade sign declaring the area "Kayla's Office." And I chuckle to myself at all of the stuffed animals and toys that inhabit her "office." Sentimental grandmother that I am, I just had to save these early e-mails from my favorite girl, all sweetly signed "Love, Kayla."
December 2004

FONT IN VERSION C

- Playful.
- Works with computer theme.
- Easy to read.

The use of all caps can make titles and journaling hard to read, especially with a complicated font. Try a few dingbats (those fun little symbols) to separate your journaling into manageable chunks.

TITLE AND JOURNALING
IN VERSION A

- Title hard to read in all caps and script.

Cache
GCB2C9

"Bye Bye
Birdy"

{GEO} *CACHING*

Wayne has a new toy—a hand-held GPS system. Purchased to help us find our way around two National Parks in the west later this year, he's been perfecting his skills in using it. So we've been geocaching—using satellite coordinates to find "treasures" hidden by others who then post the location on the internet. • The cache usually contains only trinkets; the reward is simply in fining it. Dale and Carol came along with us to look for this one, hidden along a birding trail on Dauphin Island. Dale beamed when it was his sharp eyes that spotted the cache near a tree about 10 yards off the trail. We didn't take anything from the cache but signed the log. • Sunny skies, fleeting glimpses of colorful birds and time with friends were the real treasures from this trip—and we didn't need the GPS to find them.

Version A

{geo} caching *by Brenda Arnall.* **Supplies** *Cardstock:* Bazzill Basics Paper; *Patterned paper:* BasicGrey; *Pens:* Pigma Micron, Sakura; *Font:* Zurich EX BT ("geo," subtitle and journaling), Bitstream; Brush Script MT ("caching"), Microsoft Word; *Negative transparency:* Creative Imaginations; *Wooden tag:* Chatterbox; *Decorative brad:* Making Memories.

TITLE AND JOURNALING
IN VERSION B

- Easy to read with lowercase letters.
- Dingbats within journaling break up long blocks of text.

Cache
GCB2C9

"Bye Bye
Birdy"

{geo} caching

Wayne has a new toy—a hand-held GPS system. Purchased to help us find our way around two National Parks in the west later this year, he's been perfecting his skills in using it. So we've been geocaching—using satellite coordinates to find "treasures" hidden by others who then post the location on the internet. • The cache usually contains only trinkets; the reward is simply in fining it. Dale and Carol came along with us to look for this one, hidden along a birding trail on Dauphin Island. Dale beamed when it was his sharp eyes that spotted the cache near a tree about 10 yards off the trail. We didn't take anything from the cache but signed the log. • Sunny skies, fleeting glimpses of colorful birds and time with friends were the real treasures from this trip—and we didn't need the GPS to find them.

Version B

Idea to note: Brenda downloaded and printed actual screens from the GPS system on paper, then inserted the printout in the negative transparency.

KEEP IT simple

Fonts are so much fun that it's hard to stick with just one or two. Doing so will lend a more "unified" feel to your layouts, however.

FONTS IN VERSION A

- Too many fonts, sizes and weights hurt unity and complicate look.

Version A

Stonehenge *by Brenda Arnall.* **Supplies** *Cardstock:* Bazzill Basics Paper; *Patterned paper:* Arctic Frog; *Stickers:* Chatterbox; *Pens:* Pigma Micron, Sakura; *Fonts:* Akzidenz Grotesk BE XBdCn, Arial Narrow and Minion SemiboldSC, downloaded from the Internet; CK Tea Party, "Creative Clips & Fonts for Special Occasions" CD, *Creating Keepsakes.*

type

FONTS IN VERSION B

- More unity when fonts are limited to one or two.
- Much easier on the eye.

We must have photographed every stone from every angle, we were so impressed by what we saw. But still the sun sank quickly and the tour ended too soon. There are so many good memories from our trip to England, but seeing Stonehenge at sunset remains one of my favorites.

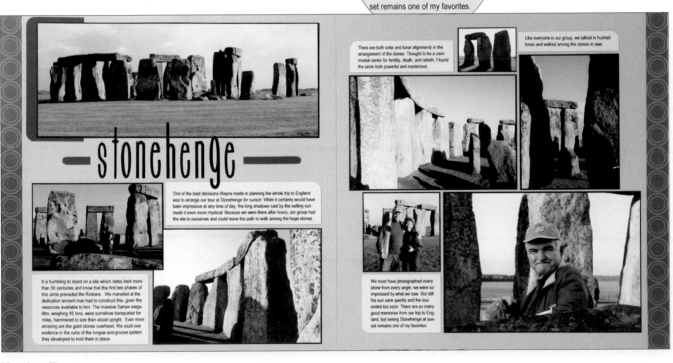

Version B

So, remember: Use upper- and lowercase letters for the greatest readability. Choose fonts that reflect the mood of your layout. Learn more about type at www.thinking-withtype.com (see page 56 for more details). You'll love what the right lettering looks can do for your layouts!

Become a Type Expert   BY ALI EDWARDS

WHAT IT'S ALL ABOUT If you've been scrapping for more than, oh, 10 minutes, you've probably discovered downloadable fonts on the Internet. I have hundreds of fonts downloaded on my computer, but how do I know which font is best for a specific layout? I visit the Thinking with Type website at www.thinkingwithtype.com! While you won't find downloadable fonts, you'll find everything else you need to get the look you want. This educational site teaches you about spacing, alignment, kerning and all the other type do's and don'ts. If you want a font history lesson, it'll give you that, too.

Another bonus? Just in case you get bored (or you're killing time before the kids come home from school), the site has "Crimes Against Typography" font games. Check out the "Dumb Quotes" game as well for an Atari-type blast from the past!

WHAT IT MEANS TO SCRAPPERS Of course you can buy the book Thinking with Type (it's terrific), but lots of info is already on the Thinking with Type website. It takes the guesswork out of tracking, font choices or choosing the most readable font for your journaling.

WHERE TO FIND IT Just go to www.thinkingwithtype.com. You can also find more educational stuff and a cool font identifier at www.linotype.com. If you're looking for free fonts, you're just a few clicks away from thousands of options. Just go to your favorite search engine (I like Google) and type in "free fonts."

After you've checked out these sites, use your search engine to look up other subjects that interest you. Just do a search. Here are some generic keywords you can look up:

- Design
- Color
- Type
- Free software
- Photography
- Journaling

Not finding what you need? Simply get more specific. Have fun! ❤

Get help—or give "Crimes Against Typography" a try!

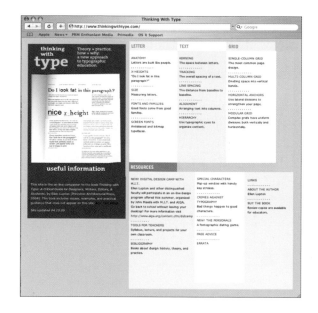

▶ **CK ONLINE**

Love being online? Don't miss Rachel Thomae's "Fun Facts on the Internet," a March 2001 article we couldn't resist pulling from the archives. Find headlines from the year you were born, famous birthdays, sports facts, zodiac signs, food facts and more. It's all at www.creatingkeepsakes.com/mag.

TO DO LiST

a way with words

Tracy

LET'S TAKE A CREATIVITY FIELD TRIP—to your kitchen pantry. Turn the cans, boxes and bags toward you. Which catches your eye first? How do the fonts, typesetting and overall presentation of the text make the package particularly effective? ❯

To-Do List *by Tracy White.* **Supplies** *Rub-ons:* BasicGrey; *Chipboard letters:* Making Memories and Scenic Route; *Computer fonts:* Eldorado Micro Roman and C-Block, Apple.

Words are just as important as photos when it comes to telling a story. And though it's not always necessary, presenting journaling in a dramatic, high-impact or whimsical way can not only make your words more eye-catching, but give them greater weight. Here, we'll explore creative approaches to text and discover ways to take journaling out of the box. Experiment to see which style will complement your next layout best!

1 *inside the lines*

I love versatility in scrapbooking. Who wouldn't love using one technique to produce several looks? This explains why I love journaling on strips. Horizontal, vertical or diagonal, on cardstock or paper, with computer-generated text, handwriting, stickers or stamps—simple strips easily adapt to suit any subject. Try this for lists (fasteners make great "bullets") hidden styles (place them in a pocket or behind a photo), or as a way to make large blocks of text more visually appealing.

2 *around the bend*

I love this effect—journaling that flows seamlessly into a layout's design by becoming one with its embellishments. Not only is this attractive, it also gives Cynthia Coulon enough room to provide details of her son's first weeks of life while keeping the focus on the adorable photos. Although Cynthia used Photoshop to add text around the large number accents, you could also handwrite or stamp text around die cuts, within shapes or along curvy paths to achieve a similar result.

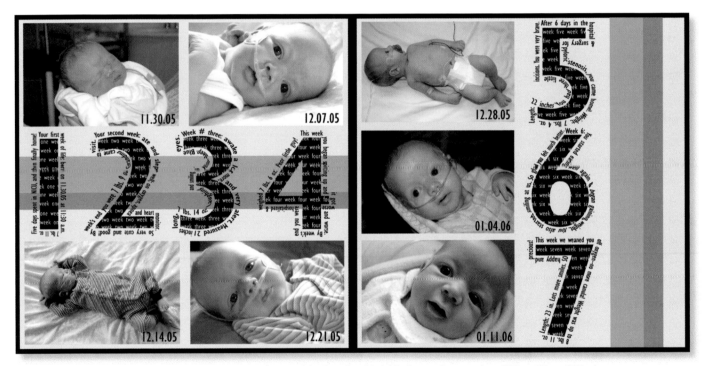

Your First Seven Weeks *by Cynthia Coulon.* **Supplies** *Computer software:* Adobe Photoshop 7.0, Adobe Systems; *Computer font:* Gill Sans, Microsoft Word.

cynthia's tips:

To add text around accents—like these numbers—I basically write a small section of text, then use the "Transform" tool to drag the text around, turn it upside-down, stretch it, angle it and otherwise make it fit where I want it. If the text needs to be curved, I use the "Warp Text" tool and write one little section at a time to make the text easier to manipulate.

3 out of bounds

As someone who needs to maximize scrapbooking time, I really appreciate this approach by Kelly Anderson. Her quick-and-easy idea simply involves handwriting text around the page's periphery. As a bonus, the journaling doubles as a funky border. Dress it up by using letter stamps, stickers or rub-ons. Or, alter the look by writing across only the top and bottom, along one side or around a photo mat or two.

New York Shopping *by Kelly Anderson.* **Supplies** *Cardstock:* WorldWin; *Rub-ons:* Making Memories; *Pens:* Gelly Roll, Sakura (white); Zig Millennium, EK Success (black); *Negative frames:* Creative Imaginations; *Label tape:* Dymo; *Tags:* Avery Dennison; *Other:* Map and bumper sticker.

4 *on the mark*

Talk about dynamic text! To commemorate her son's first guitar, Deb Perry designed a layout to resemble an artistic album cover. Using Photoshop and a digital pen, Deb imposed layers of text over her son's image for a result that's both edgy and ethereal.

If you don't scrapbook digitally, try writing or stamping directly on your photo with solvent ink—but be sure to have duplicates on hand if you're concerned about mistakes or the long-term effects on your photo.

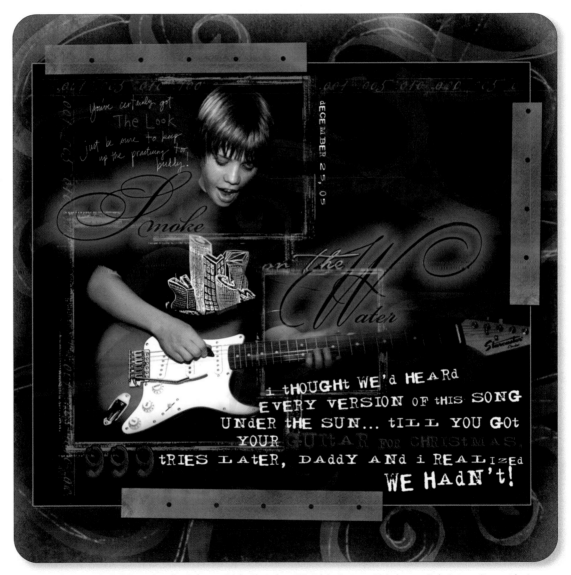

Smoke on the Water *by Deb Perry.* **Supplies** *Software:* Adobe Photoshop CS2, Adobe Systems; *Digital paper:* Early Autumn Bouquet by Jen Wilson, www.jenwilsondesigns.com; *numbers:* Black Eyed Pea Kit by Rhonna Farrer, downloaded from *www.twopeasinabucket.com; Frames:* Schmootzy Frames by Nancy Rowe Janitz, *www.scrapartist.com; Brushes:* Created by manipulating digital paper by Jen Wilson; *Computer fonts:* Facelift and Bickham Script Fancy, downloaded from the Internet; *Handwriting:* Deb's own, using a Wacom Digital Pen.

deb's digital pen tip:

The trick to writing smoothly with a digital pen is to use the zoom tool to get *very* close to the area where you want to write, usually around 100%. If your handwriting still seems shaky, just slip a piece of paper between the pen and tablet. This will increase friction and help you hold the pen steadier.

deb's text tip:

To create the journaling across the bottom of the page, I typed out the text and used a different "layer" for each line. By using "Edit > Transform > Rotate" with each line, I was able to achieve a more random look.

5 beside
the point

Don't want to add text directly to your photo? Surround the image with it instead. A kicked-up photo caption can draw attention to a favorite image and present details at the same time. Vanessa Reyes used a pretty combination of rub-on and chipboard letters, spicing things up with a variety of colors, shapes and sizes. Alter the frame to suit your layout with careful selection of fonts and elements. For a more understated look, try simple handwriting or computer-generated text. ♥

Ray of Sunshine by Vanessa Reyes. **Supplies** Patterned paper: KI Memories, Chatterbox, Petals and Possibilities and Urban Lily; Chipboard letters and shapes: Heidi Swapp for Advantus; Alphabet rub-ons, crystal brads, blossoms, metal frame, label holder, charmed enamel and staples: Making Memories; Ribbon: C.M. Offray & Son; Blue and green flower: Target.

august 04

endless **SUMMER**

nothing is better than... straight up... wildness and flip flops...with swimming hair, i love this photo of you...

wishing summer would never end. At least that carefree feeling of nowhere to go and nothing to do...but play!

endless summer

g—after a day in the pool...summer afternoon 2004

sharing the story

by HEIDI SWAPP

write it by hand

Heidi Swapp

I KNOW, you're not the biggest fan of your handwriting. It's fine for your grocery and to-do lists . . . but your scrapbook pages? You're afraid it will hurt the look or you'll mess up. Am I right?

I hope you'll reconsider. Writing some or all of your journaling adds a distinct, personal touch. It's so *you*! Here are three quick, doable solutions for improving your handwriting *today*. ⟩

Endless Summer by Heidi Swapp. **Supplies** Decorative tape, chipboard theme, chipboard shapes, mini tag, rub-on letters and jewels: Heidi Swapp for Advantus; Ribbon: Making Memories and May Arts; Other: Silk flower.

3 scrapbookers take the challenge

Writing by hand can seem hard. What if you forget a word or run out of space? What if your sentences run uphill or downhill? What if your journaling is lengthy and you're short on time? You'll find help here, along with sample pages by yours truly (that's me!), Pam Kopka and Veronica Ponce.

SOLUTION 1:

use pencil

I'm always surprised at how many scrapbookers pick up a pen and start journaling without preparing first. Don't do it! Jot down first on scratch paper what you want to say, then pencil in your words and reread them before committing pen to page. You can then concentrate fully on how the writing looks.

Here, Pam Kopka did freeform journaling on a layout about a painful topic. "I found it very therapeutic," says Pam, "and in many ways it captured the emotions I was feeling. Still, I knew that a few inconsistencies could be distracting, so I did a second version where I drew in lines, letters and baselines first. I always do this when I need my writing to be most uniform."

HEIDI

PAM

VERONICA

More Help from Heidi

Love Heidi and her handwriting? You'll find hundreds of tips and ideas in her book, *Love Your Handwriting*. Learn to create your own "fonts." Discover a surprisingly handy tool for exact spacing. Try new title effects. Create "voluptuous" letters. You'll get excited about writing again with this cool book and workbook. Not only that—you'll receive a starter set of writing tools. $29.95. To order, visit *www.creatingkeepsakes.com/shop*.

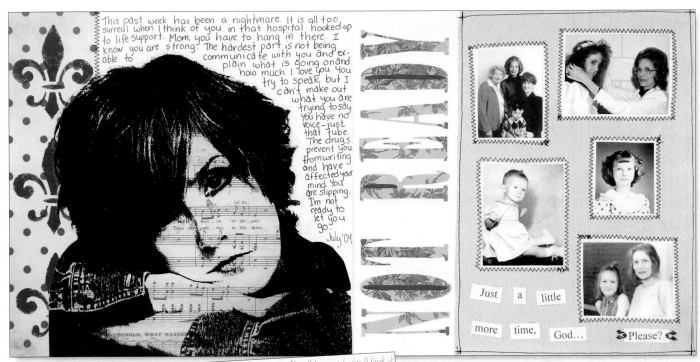

This past week has been a nightmare. It is all too surreal when I think of you in that hospital hooked-up to life support. Mom, you have to hang in there. I know you are strong. The hardest part is not being able to communicate with you and explain what is going on and how much I love you. You try to speak, but I can't make out what you are trying to say. You have no voice—just that tube. The drugs prevent you from writing and have affected your mind. You are slipping. I'm not ready to let you go. July '04

NOT READY

Just a little more time, God... Please?

Just a Little More Time *by Pam Kopka.*
Supplies *Patterned papers:* Daisy D's Paper Co.; *Transparency:* Artistic Expressions; *Computer font:* Times New Roman, Microsoft Word; *Pen:* American Crafts; *Other:* Tulle and teardrop sticker. *Ideas to note:* Pam used a fine-tip pen to write more precisely on the variation. The lyrics are part of the patterned-paper design.

> *Tip:* Write ever so lightly and use a white eraser—not the flesh-colored variety—to erase mistakes without smudging.

> *Tip:* Hold your "planning" paper up to a computer screen, light box or window to help determine space and fit.

> *Tip:* Proofread your text for misspellings or omissions before going over it with pen.

> *Tip:* Keep the spacing between words similar—it will look cleaner and be easier to read.

SOLUTION 2:

watch size and shape

Take your time! As you write, concentrate on making each letter approximately the same size and shape. Keep lower-case letters the same height.

To help on letter shape, imagine you've got a row of text boxes lined up: (just like you'd see on a credit card application). The boxes might be square—or they might be tall rectangles or long rectangles. Note how they all provide the same amount of space to fill. Visualize keeping each letter in its imaginary "box" as you draw it.

SOLUTION 3:

remember—it's not "all or nothing"

A little handwriting goes a long way! If you have a lot to say, type most of your message on the computer and accent with hand-lettering like Veronica Ponce did in the second version at right. (Isn't this a cool page? A friend showed it to me online.)

Write directly on the layout or, if you're a digital scrap-booker, scan the words you've written and place them electronically.

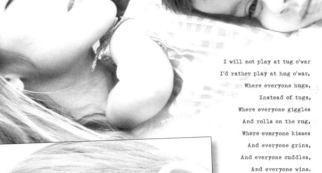

I will not play at tug o'war
I'd rather play at hug o'war,
Where everyone hugs,
Instead of tugs,
Where everyone giggles
And rolls on the rug,
Where everyone kisses
And everyone grins,
And everyone cuddles,
And everyone wins.

> *Tip:* Handwrite a few words for a more personal feel. (See below.)

> *Tip:* Accent your handwriting with stickers, embellishments or stamps.

> *Tip:* Overlap your journaling and title for variety. ❤

I will not play at tug o'war
I'd rather play at hug o'war,
Where everyone *hugs*,
Instead of tugs,
Where everyone giggles
And *rolls* on the rug,
Where everyone *kisses*,
And everyone grins,
And everyone cuddles,
And everyone *wins*.

Hug O' War *by Veronica Ponce.* **Supplies** *Computer font:* Love Letter, downloaded from the Internet; *Poem:* Adapted from "Hug O' War" by Shel Silverstein.

ck hot spot

by LORI FAIRBANKS

notebook paper

LOOK AT TODAY'S MAGAZINES and websites, and you'll note a popular trend: handwritten or printed text on scraps of notebook paper. Translate this look to scrapbooking for a no-fuss, no-frills journaling approach that's hard to resist! Check out this page by Joanna Bolick, then use notebook paper on your next page. ❤

Use notebook paper to convey the feeling of jotting a fleeting thought. *Harper by Joanna Bolick.* **Supplies** *Patterned papers:* Making Memories, me & my BIG ideas and Sandylion; *Notebook paper:* Mead; *Flower accents:* Heidi Swapp for Advantus; *Rub-on quote:* 7gypsies; *Pens:* Uni-ball, Sanford.

Consider notebook, ledger and graph paper from the following companies:

❶ 7gypsies
www.7gypsies.com

❷ Creative Imaginations
www.cigift.com

❸ Hot Off The Press
www.paperwishes.com

❹ Making Memories
www.makingmemories.com

❺ Karen Foster Design
www.karenfosterdesign.com

practice your penmanship

REMEMBER LEARNING TO WRITE in elementary school? You know, tracing letters on specially lined paper and following shapes to create the same straight lines and rounded letters? ❯

So She Said . . . by Tracy White. **Supplies** *Patterned paper and rubons:* SEI; *Paper ribbon:* Idea inspired by Mi'Chelle Larsen's "Singing Bird" layout in *Can-Do Techniques* by *Creating Keepsakes; Computer font:* Swiss, Apple Computer; *Other:* Transparency.

Over the years, people's penmanship tends to develop a unique flair. Mine, I'm sad to say, is not fresh. Or cool. It can even be downright messy. Nevertheless, my penmanship is an extension of my personality—and what flows when I put a pen in hand. Wouldn't future generations want this glimpse of me regardless of what the letters look like?

I think they would, so here's a penmanship assignment for you. Design a few layouts that will showcase your handwriting and that of your friends and family. Whether that handwriting is beautiful, unusual or barely legible, it's important to preserve what it looks like for your family history.

1 *parents*

Luckily, I don't "judge" the handwriting of my family and friends the way I do mine. Instead, I keep all the letters and cards they send because I don't want to lose that piece of them. My favorites are the ones from Mom—just seeing her writing instantly takes me home. I'd recognize her writing anywhere.

Seek out your parents' handwriting in a variety of places like birthday cards, notes or gift tags. Incorporate it on your pages as a sentimental touch.

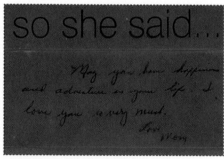

I scanned an excerpt from a card my mom gave me, then printed it on a transparency to preserve it.

hate your handwriting?

You've seen "cute" handwriting. Mine is not. My letters run into each other and my signature is, well, barely legible. Its appearance definitely holds me back from journaling by hand. Are you the same way? Perhaps these tips from Heidi Swapp's book *Love Your Handwriting* will build confidence!

- **Start with scratch paper.** Think about what you want to say and write it on scratch paper first. This lets you form complete thoughts, cross out words or start over. You can determine how much space you'll need—no more words crammed together!

- **Reverse the process.** Instead of designing the page first, journal, *then* decide where to place each element. When you start with a blank canvas, you won't have the fear of "messing up" a perfect page.

- **Find the perfect pen and paper.** Your perfect match could be a marker, roller ball or calligraphy pen. Try it on different weights and textures of cardstock. Discover what makes your writing look its best.

- **Start small.** Take small steps by combining your writing with computer fonts, adding text on tags (that you can redo easily if necessary) or on smaller projects like cards.

- **Discover your style.** Study computer fonts, magazine text and product packaging to see what lettering treatments you love. Try incorporating the styles into your handwriting.

I am ~~afraid~~ fearless

I am ~~silent~~ heard

I am ~~weak~~ strong

I am a ~~coward~~ brave

I am ~~unmotivated~~ driven

I am ~~dependant~~ independant

I am ~~unsure~~ confident

I am ~~insignificant~~ valuable

I am 31. I am finally free from a past that has haunted me and defined much of my life. If i have ever felt a true turning point than this year has been it. I am determined to live a better life.

Redefined by Jenni Bowlin. **Supplies** *Patterned paper:* Chatterbox; *Rub-ons:* Heidi Swapp for Advantus; *Computer font:* Courier New, Microsoft Word; *Other:* Rhinestones, metal trim and flower from a hair clip.

2 *yourself*

Though I'm reluctant to write on my own pages, seeing the richness and personality it adds could change my mind. Jenni Bowlin's handwriting here gives the page more poignancy and meaning than a slew of fonts would have. As a tip for those too intimidated to inscribe all of the text, Jenni suggests mixing fonts with a few handwritten words as a small, personal touch.

Thank You *by Laurie Stamas.* **Supplies** *Patterned paper:* Li'l Davis Designs; *Fabric letters:* Making Memories; *Stamping ink:* ColorBox, Clearsnap; *Pens:* Pigma Micron (black) and Sharpie (white), Sanford; *Clips and chipboard piece:* Heidi Swapp for Advantus; *Brad:* Bazzill Basics Paper; *Rub-on stitches:* Autumn Leaves; *Other:* Ribbon, thread and twill.

3 *friends*

In school, writing notes was a popular way to endure a "boring" lecture or share some gossip. But as we get older, we communicate on the phone or at long lunches, forgoing the notes we used to love. When Laurie Stamas recently received a note from her friend, she knew it was something to treasure. Enhance layouts about your friends with letters you've exchanged.

Impressions of Kyoto *by Lisa Brown Caveney.* **Supplies** *Pen:* Uni-ball Signo, Sanford; *Computer fonts:* AL Sandra, "15 Handwritten Fonts" CD, Autumn Leaves; Arial, Microsoft Word; *Other:* Origami paper.

4 *significant other*

If you've ever had one of those "he said, she said" moments, a layout noting both sides can be an insightful way to document it. When Lisa Brown Caveney and her husband visited Japan on work-related trips *one week apart*, a layout—featuring each of their hand-written accounts—reveals their individual impressions perfectly. Hand your spouse the pen from time to time for a unique point of view in your family albums.

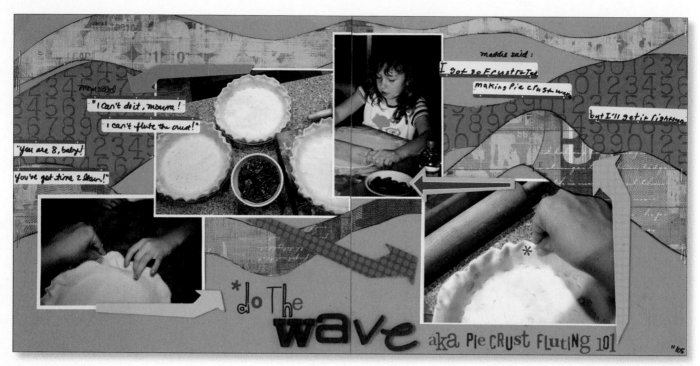

Do the Wave *by Terrie McDaniel.* **Supplies** *Patterned papers:* KI Memories and BasicGrey; *Rub-ons, chipboard and acrylic accents:* KI Memories; *Folder labels:* Avery Dennison. ❤

5 *children*

I changed my handwriting constantly as I went through school. If your kids are the same, be sure to record each stage of the transformation. Scrapbook the notes they write to you or add snippets of essays and tests from school. Better yet, have your kids write captions for your pages, as Terrie McDaniel did with her daughter. Memories of moments spent with Mom gain meaning when recounted in Maddie's own hand. ❤

When I travel, I always want to see it all.

The big attractions. The famous spots. Even the not-so-obvious local treasures.

I love to take in every sight that makes a city special.

Mom got this picture of me on a bus in Sydney. I love that it captures me sketching out a map & planning where to go next... and my desire to

see it all.

See it all...

Sydney · 08·2005

jennifer

sweet solution

Use That Space

Ever have photos with lots of dark space? Instead of cropping it off, leave the space intact and use a white pen to add a title or journaling. If you aren't thrilled with your handwriting, add the words in Photoshop, then trace with a pen after printing.

—Jennifer McGuire, Cincinnati, OH

See It All *by Jennifer McGuire.* **Supplies** *Patterned papers:* American Crafts; *Brads:* Accent Depot; *Flowers:* Prima; *Corner punch:* EK Success; *White pen:* Sharpie, Sanford; *Computer font:* 2Peas A Beautiful Mess, downloaded from *www.twopeasinabucket.com.*

Daily Thoughts

Share what's on your mind

We scrapbookers are always taking photos! Yet how often do we take an *internal* snapshot of our lives and scrapbook it? You know, like recording the little thoughts that fill our minds and say so much about us, but which family members may never know if we don't record them?

These thoughts reveal our interests, our personalities and how we look at the world. They're the things you wish you'd known about your great-grandmother to better understand her and her life. How cool would that be? Very. That's how your family and future generations will react, too, if you scrapbook *your* internal snapshot.

Now, I know you're busy and have plenty of layouts to scrapbook. But I also know your family would treasure a layout like this. Create a "daily thoughts" layout today!

by Becky Higgins

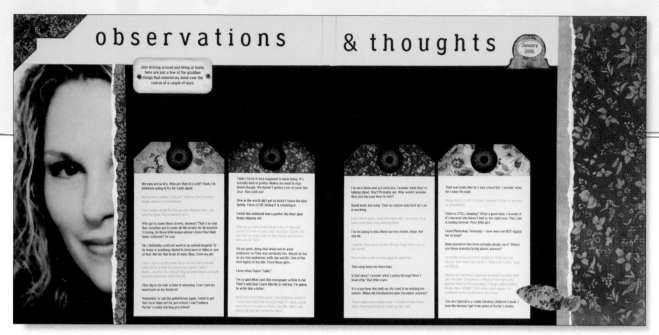

Observations & Thoughts by Becky Higgins. **Supplies** *Textured cardstock:* Bazzill Basics Paper; *Patterned papers, decorative accents and tag tops:* Daisy D's Paper Co.; *Epoxy accent:* Making Memories; *Brads:* Boxer Scrapbook Productions; *Chalk:* Stampin' Up!; *Computer font:* Clique-Serif, downloaded from the Internet.

The Challenge

Here's my challenge to you: Carry a small notebook or recording device wherever you go for one day. Every time you get a minute, jot down notes about the thoughts passing through your mind. Don't worry about grammar, spelling or sentence structure. Don't try to think about anything in particular. Just let your mind do its thing. Whether you're hanging out at home, working at the office, waiting at a stoplight or standing in a line doesn't matter. Just record.

At the end of the day, look at your notes or listen to your audio. Document the thoughts before they start fading away! Spend a few extra moments to jot down the context of each thought as well. (Where were you at 7:52 that made you think about XYZ? What first triggered the thought chain you had at 4:26?) Of course you know the next step: scrapbook those thoughts! Include pictures from that particular day, a current picture of you or even no pictures at all.

Once you've tried this, get the family involved! Ask your husband or boyfriend, parents, older kids or friends to take on this assignment. I asked my dad, my friend Amy and my son to take the challenge with me. I love the results!

Jot down notes about the thoughts passing through your mind.

4:21 am • It's morning already? Whew! No alarm for another half hour.

5:11 am • No way...I slept in AGAIN?!?

5:15 am • I wonder what kind of fish those are supposed to be on the shower curtain. Are there even real fish that look like that?

5:26 am • Cute or comfy? I just did laundry...how 'bout a happy medium? Let's go with a collared shirt and my favorite jeans.

6:09 am • Is there REALLY a market for this music?

7:01 am • The Star Spangled Banner a capella is a dangerous venture. Who is this singing? Excellent pitch. I'm impressed!

7:10 am • Yes! Sit-ups yesterday, Wheaties this morning...that definitely compensates for my stash of Samoas upstairs.

7:27 am • Those orange construction barrels have been there forever. It's so annoying how they just sit there in the middle of the road!

7:48 am • T-minus four months till graduation!

9:24 am • Torque...uh, fork...pork...

12:05 pm • I hate calculus. It takes so long, and who needs integrals, anyway?

12:46 pm • I should NOT use that granola bar wrapper as a bookmark. It makes me way too hungry.

1:14 pm • Thank you, Adam Smith. Capitalism rocks, and no, WalMart will not take over the world.

1:42 pm • What? Snow in January? In *Cleveland*???

2:23 pm • I should tap into my creative talents more often. Stop thinking inside the box!!

3:08 pm • Those flowers are so beautiful! I should grow a garden sometime.

7:12 pm • I wonder how microphones work?

9:34 pm • Work *tomorrow*, too? That's over 20 hours this week! $$$

10:18 pm • Mmm...pineapple is definitely my favorite fruit.

Tuesday, January 24th in the year 2006. This is what crosses my mind in the course of a day.

Another life in the day of Amy.

Amy *by Becky Higgins, journaling by Amy Barwick.* **Supplies** *Textured cardstock:* Bazzill Basics Paper; *Monogram letter:* BasicGrey; *Computer font:* SimplexLight, downloaded from the Internet; *Other:* Thread.

Turn your thoughts into a daily planner of sorts by noting the time each came to mind. This can enhance the page flow of your otherwise random observations. Plus, it's a terrific insight into how your thoughts progressed throughout the day.

You can still include the context of each thought with the time. Or, leave it out to add a whimsical feel and make viewers wonder, "How in the world did she come up with that?!" I'd be curious to know about some of Amy's statements!

When to Pull Out That Pen

Prefer structure to complete freedom? Add a little regimen to your note-taking. Instead of recording your thoughts at random moments, consider jotting them down at these intervals:

• Every 30, 45 or 60 minutes

• When someone walks by wearing a certain color of shirt

• At meals and each time you grab a snack

• Every time you catch yourself daydreaming

• Any time you participate in a given task

• Whenever you walk into a new room

• Whenever you hear a certain word

• When someone sneezes nearby

MY MIND

What's on my mind in the course of 48 hours
Late January 2006
By Wayne Allgaier

Lying in bed after the alarm clock goes off • This is my long day at the office. I'll be seeing patients from 8:30 am until 9:30 pm, then three or four hours returning phone calls, phoning in prescriptions, and reviewing test results. Hopefully I'll have a little time at lunchtime and dinner time to return a few of the more urgent phone calls, but I'll probably spend that time seeing extra patients that will be worked in. I'll come back tomorrow on my "day off" and spend four or five hours catching up on paperwork. We need another doctor in the practice!

[Short version]: How am I possibly going to get everything done today that needs to be done?

Lunchtime • Lunch is never an option – thank goodness for SlimFast – but I thought I might be able to return a few of the more urgent phone calls at noon. Instead, I spent the hour seeing additional patients that had to be seen. We need another doctor!

While working with a new computer system at the office • We've been using this system for four months. We're past the major part of the learning curve. And it's still taking us at least 50% longer to do what we were doing before. I guess this is the wave of the future, but I'm glad I'll be retiring soon and getting away from it. I feel sorry for my younger partners who have many years to work with it.

While waiting for the ambulance to take me to the hospital • This nosebleed has come at a very inconvenient time. I have about 20 patients waiting to be seen, and they will have to call in my partners, who are enjoying what little time they have at home to come in and see these patients.

Following a trip to the emergency room for a severe nosebleed • Isn't it great to live in an age where we have the technology to take care of our medical emergencies? I reflect back on several instances in my life and in the lives of other members of our family where this has been the case.

The day after the nosebleed, when I'm feeling better • Okay, I really appreciate all the attention people are giving me, but I really would like to get on with life, and they won't let me.

Sitting in the dentist chair waiting to have the crown of a new tooth to be inserted, the final step of a lengthy and expensive process • This tooth better feel good and it better match the adjacent teeth, as much as I'm paying for it!

Contemplating my responsibilities as Chairman of the downtown revitalization effort • I thought when I 'cut back' my office hours four months ago I would have more time to devote to this and other projects. I'm down to a 55 hour work week, and there is still very little time. I wish I could retire altogether, but that can't happen until we find a replacement for me.

On a rare warm beautiful day when I had to spend the day at the office catching up on paper work • I would give anything to be out working in the yard today. What's wrong with this picture?

Sitting on the airplane beside a very friendly and talkative stranger • This guy sure is friendly, but I value my airplane trips as time away from the phone and people where I can catch up on reading and other projects that I never seem to have time for at home. Why can't he find something to read?!

Dead tired, going to bed • Ahhh, it feels *so good* to stretch out in the horizontal position. This bed is *so* comfortable!!

Contemplating Becky's assignment for me to write down my "random thoughts" during the day • This is an impossible task. I have about a zillion thoughts go through my head every day. How do I write them all down?!" I guess I have been successful in capturing a few of them, and this has been an insightful experience for me.

My Mind *by Becky Higgins, journaling by Wayne Allgaier.* **Supplies** *Textured cardstock:* Bazzill Basics Paper; *Wood letters:* Li'l Davis Designs; *Photo turns:* Making Memories; *Metallic brads:* Die Cuts With a View; *Photo corners:* Heidi Swapp for Advantus; *Computer font:* Garamond, Microsoft Word.

Jot down your thoughts based on a particular theme.

Once you start writing down your thoughts, you may notice a trend that seems to appear on a given day (or week!). Since it's impossible to write down every thought, once you find a theme, stick with it and simply record the applicable musings. That seems doable, even for a busy mom like me!

8 Thought Starters

Jot down your thoughts based on a particular theme, such as:

- A loved one
- Food cravings
- Upcoming plans
- What appears in the media
- Thoughts about your environment
- A recent or soon-to-air TV show
- Memories that make you laugh
- Points you want to ponder later

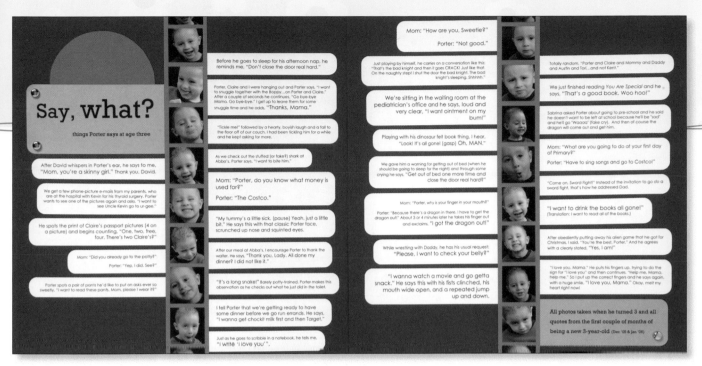

Say, What? *by Becky Higgins.* **Supplies** *Textured cardstock:* Bazzill Basics Paper; *Brads:* Making Memories; *Computer fonts:* Rockwell (title), downloaded from the Internet; Century Gothic (journaling), Microsoft Word.

Wondering about recording the random thoughts of children who are too young to write? Record the things they say throughout the day! Include any actions or body language as well to help capture the fullness of each quote. If some things were said "out of the blue," note them to emphasize the wonder and innocence behind the young thoughts.

4 Reasons to Involve Your Children

Undertake this exercise with children, and you'll love the results! Here are the top four reasons I'm all for doing it:

1 Kids often say exactly what they're thinking. You may find yourself chuckling as you put their thoughts on paper.

2 You'll be amazed at the window into your child's life these little sayings provide.

3 Children grow up *way* too fast! Be sure to record their cute little phrases so you won't forget them in the future.

4 You'll love it when the little ones don't know you're listening. The results can be quite charming and amusing! ♥

Uniform Doodles

Doodling is all the rage, yet some people like to have more symmetrical doodles than others. A stencil is a great way to ensure that your circles, arrowheads or journaling boxes are even if you want that look. ♥

—*Sande Krieger, Salt Lake City, UT*

The Boys Hit Paris *by Sande Krieger.*
Supplies *Textured cardstock:* Bazzill Basics Paper and Provo Craft; *Patterned paper and tag:* Making Memories; *Chipboard letters and bookplates:* Li'l Davis Designs; *Stamping ink:* ColorBox, Clearsnap; *Rubber stamps:* Impress Rubber Stamps and Postmodern Design; *Brads:* Making Memories and Creative Impressions; *Journaling strip:* 7gypsies; *Ribbon:* May Arts; *Copper star:* Nunn Design; *Glitter circles:* Jesse James & Co.; *Silhouette word:* Heidi Swapp for Advantus; *Rub-ons:* Memories Complete; *Stencil:* The C-Thru Ruler Co.; *Adhesive:* Therm O Web; *Other:* Glass diamonds.

For easy doodling, use stencils!

capture life | create art

remember me

by ALI EDWARDS

photo by ANDREA LIPSTEIN

When I first started scrapbooking in 2002, my son was 11 months old and I'd been accumulating "stuff" since his birth. Scrapbooking seemed to be the perfect match between organizing that "stuff" and telling his story. >

Now, almost five years later, one of the greatest effects scrapbooking has had on my life is that I'm now telling my own story as well. It's become a big part of what I do.

Many scrapbookers remark, "I barely have time to do my kids' books—why would I spend time on me?" This is why:

• Because it's fun.

• Because you are worth it.

• Because your kids will want to know about you.

• Because it's therapeutic and helps you figure out what makes you tick.

• Because it's healthy to take time to do something just for you.

• Because no one can tell your story better than you.

Your story doesn't have to be super-long. It doesn't need to include every detail of your life. Look at it as an opportunity to put into your own words the way you see the world, your experiences, your celebrations and the bits of your life that are important to you.

Here are five ideas for layouts that will tell the key parts of your story:

• Remember Me

• This I Believe

• My Hope

• What I Need

• Why [Someone] Is Special to Me

Remember Me *by Ali Edwards.* **Supplies** *Cardstock:* Bazzill Basics Paper; *Patterned paper:* Scenic Route; *Tab punch:* McGill; *Letter stickers, rub-ons and pen:* American Crafts; *Hearts:* Heidi Swapp for Advantus; *Paint:* Making Memories.

Ali's notes

> Stick with the "Remember Me" theme and journal a short bit near each photo that begins with the sentiment.

> One of my favorite products right now is McGill's Mini File Tab punch. I love that I can pick any paper and create my own tabs in an instant. Use adhesive or staples to keep them in place.

This I Believe by Ali Edwards. **Supplies** *Cardstock:* Bazzill Basics Paper; *Patterned paper, black frame stickers and circle sticker:* 7gypsies; *Pen:* American Crafts; *Letter stamps:* PSX Design; *Circle stamp:* Autumn Leaves; *Circle punch:* Punch Bunch.

Ali's notes

> I'm a collector of things that resonate with me. The bits and pieces on this layout came directly off the bulletin board that sits above my computer. This layout is the perfect place for them. Look around your home. Do you see any bits and pieces that share what you believe? What could you use on your layout?

> Be sure to add a bit of explanation about items on tags or tabs.

> Scrapbooking doesn't have to be neat and tidy. Life isn't neat and tidy. Create pages that reflect your perspective or your emotional state.

The "This I Believe" idea comes straight from National Public Radio. According to its website, "This I Believe" is "based on a 1950's radio program of the same name, [where] Americans from all walks of life share the personal philosophies and core values that guide their daily lives." You can read more about it online (and contribute your own essay as well) at *http://www.npr.org/templates/story/story.php?storyId=4538138*.

> For a cool title, attach a transparency to your layout with two brads and add adhesive chipboard letters.

> Take color cues from your photos. When I looked at my scanned layout in a photo-editing program, I could see that the page still needed a couple of elements. Pulling some of the red-orange and the light-blue colors from the photo, I added the swirl stamp (repeating the swirl on the transparency) and the small red rub-ons to finish up the layout.

Detail your hopes for someone you love. The "My Hope" text can be long or short, simple or complex—just make sure it's in your own words.

My Hope by Ali Edwards. **Supplies** *Patterned papers:* KI Memories and Making Memories; *Chipboard letters:* Heidi Swapp for Advantus; *Transparency:* My Mind's Eye; *Rub-ons:* 7gypsies; *Stamp:* FontWerks; *Ink:* VersaColor, Tsukineko; *Font:* ATF Antique, downloaded from the Internet.

I've wanted to do a page like this for a long time—where I crop images from magazines and mix them in with photos and other ephemera from around my home. This is a great way to gather up a collection of your personal "needs." Some of the items are totally "excess" and others are "essential"—but they are all me. And that's what I'm after as I tell my story.

I Need by Ali Edwards. **Supplies** *Cardstock:* Bazzill Basics Paper; *Letter stickers:* Scenic Route; *Rub-ons;* Daisy D's Paper Co.; *Stamps:* FontWerks (circle) and PSX Design; *Pen:* American Crafts; *Stamping ink:* Stampin' Up!; *Font:* 1942 Report, downloaded from the Internet; *Other:* Cork paper.

> I don't think I'll ever grow tired of my square punch. It's one of my most essential tools, and I love it.

> The "I Need" concept is a great one to add to a list of "pages to do again in another year." Some things will remain the same while others will change.

the story
i am just so...lucky

there are a million and one reasons why the two of you are SPECIAL to me. Today I looked through iPhoto and came across these from December 2006. The color is off...but the sentiment is perfect. TWO BOYS being silly and goofy and having fun together. Experiencing life together. Just being...without obligations and responsibilities. I love it. I love you both. Always

Special by Ali Edwards. **Supplies** *Cardstock:* Bazzill Basics Paper; *Patterned papers:* American Crafts, KI Memories and Sassafras Lass; *Rub-ons:* Daisy D's Paper Co.; *Chipboard accents:* Imagination Project; *Date sticker:* 7gypsies; *Pen:* American Crafts.

We all have special people in our lives. Create a layout that documents some of their best qualities in your words. I'll bet you can find photos to match! ❤

Ali's notes

> Grab three patterned papers and get to work. Here, each of the papers is from a different manufacturer but they're all linked by the color red.

I WILL NEVER FORGET
I WILL ALWAYS
I LOVE
I THINK
I CAN
WE HAVE SO MUCH FUN

ILLUSTRATION © MARYN ROOS

mix&
MATCH

3 super-easy ways to add

journaling to your pages

When my daughter Jaeme was two, I tried to pick out a cute outfit for her each day and was told—loudly—that she could "dress her own self!" The struggle was resolved when I discovered a rack of mix-and-match clothing at my favorite children's store. Imagine—all the tops matched all the pants, no matter what combination my daughter selected. Sure, Jaeme still wore an occasional top inside-out, but at least her outfits *looked* coordinated.

I've recently discovered that mix-and-match journaling can be just as liberating and stress-reducing as color-coded clothing. Give these options a try!

BY RACHEL THOMAE

the mix-and-match method

Ready to journal? Select one or two of these options.
Each can stand alone—or mix and match as desired.

a. the quote

- Start with a quote that expresses how you feel about the photographs on your page or helps summarize the story on your layout.

- Use your own words—or check out websites such as Quoteland (*www.quoteland.com*) or the Quotations Page (*www.quotationspage.com*).

- Consider quotes from children's books, favorite movies, advertisements or other places.

b. the sentence starter

- Start with an "I" statement. For example, "I feel," "I remember," "I think," "I will never forget" or "I have always . . ."

- Complete your thoughts in a single sentence. For example, "I will never forget the Christmas when you refused to open your gifts."

- Be creative. Start your sentence with any combination of words that helps tell your story. For example, "As I looked out the window . . ." or "When the door locked behind me, I realized . . ." You'll find more sentence starters in the sidebar on page 92.

c. the conversation

- Start by recalling cute, funny, silly or serious conversations with family members or friends.

- Jot down specific words exchanged during the conversation.

- Ask family members to chat with you about the events you're scrapbooking.

the mix-and-match method, illustrated

I recently challenged six scrapbookers to take the mix-and-match journaling challenge. See what they came up with, then match up your results!

Believe *by Leora Sanford.* **Supplies** *Digital paper and embellishments:* Downloaded from *www.digitaldesignessentials.com; Fonts:* Pharmacy and Century Gothic, downloaded from the Internet.

a. quote

• Leora started her journaling with one of her favorite quotes.

• She framed a portion of her daughter's photograph with the quote.

• **MATCH IT!** Create a border or frame with a favorite quote.

Two *by Wendy Sue Anderson.* **Supplies** *Patterned paper, cardstock, chipboard shapes, letter stickers, number stickers, rub-ons and ribbon:* Making Memories; *Accent clip:* Doodlebug Design; *Pen:* American Crafts; *Circle cutter:* EK Success.

b. sentence starter

- Wendy started her journaling with the words "I think . . ."

- She finished her sentence with a few words about her son's birthday.

- **MATCH IT!** Journal your thoughts directly onto strips of cardstock.

10 sentence starters

Want more ideas for journaling option B? These sentence starters will help you tell your story in no time at all!

1. The minute I closed the door, I knew . . .

2. It seemed like an ordinary Monday until . . .

3. The only thing I could think of to say was . . .

4. She was running toward me and . . .

5. We had so much fun when . . .

6. He laughed so hard that . . .

7. I couldn't believe it when . . .

8. I hadn't planned to be . . .

9. She always says . . .

10. The party was . . .

dinner conversation with a rock star

Evynn 5yrs 2006

you: Hey mom, don't I totally look like a teenager tonight?
me: Sure, babe, you sure do. I like your shirt
you: I'm wearing my biker boots and my hat, too...do you think I look like I could go hang at the mall with my friends?.

me: Uhhhm...I think maybe you're a little young to hang at the mall with your friends.
you: Oh, ok. Well, I guess I'll just be a rock star instead.
me: Good plan, good plan (trying to hide laughter)

Dinner with a Rock Star *by Jenn Olson.* **Supplies** *Software:* Adobe Photoshop CS2, Adobe Systems; *Digital patterned paper and embellishments.* Nancie Rowe Janitz and Michelle Coleman, *www.scrapartist.com; Fonts:* Petita Medium and Petita Bold, downloaded from the Internet.

c. conversation

- Jenn started her journaling by remembering a cute conversation with her daughter.
- She wrote her journaling as a back-and-forth dialogue.
- **MATCH IT!** Record a favorite conversation on a border strip.

a+c = quote and conversation

- Joanna started her journaling with an appropriate quote from *Where the Wild Things Are,* a children's book by Maurice Sendak.
- She added a short conversation she had with her son about his Halloween costume.
- **MIX IT!** Start with your page title and add a supporting quote.

Wild Things *by Joanna Bolick.* **Supplies** *Cardstock:* Bazzill Basics Paper; *Patterned paper:* BasicGrey, Cosmo Cricket and Chatterbox; *Rub-ons and stickers:* Making Memories and Heidi Grace Designs; *Digital kit:* Well Worn by Erica Hernandez, *www.twopeasinabucket.com; Fonts:* Adobe Jensen Pro and NewsGothicMT, downloaded from the Internet; *Other:* White pen.

I Like *by Jamie Waters.* **Supplies** *Cardstock:* Bazzill Basics Paper; *Rub-on letters:* Autumn Leaves; *Embellishments:* KI Memories and Making Memories.

b+c = sentence starter and conversation

• Jamie started her journaling with an "I like" statement from her son.

• She added a conversation that explains why her son likes to take his stuffed bear to school with him.

• MIX IT! Prompt the subject of your photo to tell you a bit more with an "I remember" statement.

"To the world you just may be **one person,** but to one person, you may be **the world**"

~ *Josephine Billings*

Watching my husband talk to our daughter...makes me fall in love with him all over again (and again, and again, and again).

World *by Lisa Russo.* **Supplies** *Patterned paper:* Kaleidoscope, My Mind's Eye; *Fonts:* Falstaff Serifa BT, Clarissa and VistaSansBlack, all downloaded from the Internet.

b+a = sentence starter and quote

• Lisa started her journaling with the words "Watching my husband talk to our daughter . . ."

• She added a quote that relates to the shared bond between her daughter and husband.

• **MIX IT!** Ask all the subjects featured on your layout to finish the same story starter—you'll have a fun perspective on how they viewed the event. ♥

10 favorite quotes

Say a lot with a little — by Marianne Madsen

Paired with the right photo and personal journaling, a quote can add the perfect finishing touch to a page. Here are a few of our favorites.

I wish I could show you, when you are lonely or in darkness, the astonishing light of your own being.

—Hafiz

I've learned that no matter how serious your life requires you to be, everyone needs a friend to act goofy with.

—Andy Rooney

Be who you are and say what you feel, because those who mind don't matter and those who matter don't mind.

—Dr. Seuss

Some family trees bear an enormous crop of nuts.

—Unknown

Friends are the sunshine of life.

—John Hay

We can choose to make our love for each other what our lives are really about.

—Werner Erhard

If we did all the things we are capable of, we would astound ourselves!

—Thomas Edison

Do one thing every day that scares you.

—Eleanor Roosevelt

Babies are such a nice way to start people.

—Don Herrold

You can learn many things from children. How much patience you have, for instance.

—Franklin P. Jones

Try these 10 web sites for more inspiring quotes:

- www.annabelle.net
- www.brainyquotes.com
- www.inspirationpeak.com
- www.terimartin.com
- www.quotegallery.com
- www.quotegarden.com
- www.quoteland.com
- www.quotationspage.com
- www.worldofquotes.com
- www.famous-quotations.com

Copies permitted—or just cut the quotes out and use them! ❤

PHOTO © ELSIE FLANNIGAN

Be Real, Be You

Capture your "essence" on your pages

When I finish a layout, I don't ask myself, "Is this layout good enough?" Instead, I ask, "Is this layout me?" Years from now, that's all that will really matter! I can add my personality to my pages in many ways, from what I write in my journaling to the design elements I use.

How can you make a layout "you"? How can you be real in your albums? As a scrapbook artist, I think you should be free to create in the way that best expresses *you*. Here's how I put myself in my layouts—and how you can do the same with yours!

by ELSIE FLANNIGAN

REAL JOURNALING

My journaling is an honest snapshot of who I am today, including my hopes (baby fever!), my beliefs (soul mates!) and fun peeks into my daily life (I really could live on sushi and smoothies!).

REAL PHOTOGRAPHS

Having your picture taken with your eyes closed can be a vulnerable experience—but it can also capture a side not seen when you're worrying about saying "cheese" for the photographer.

REAL DESIGN

My favorite part of scrapbooking is the playing! On this layout, I framed my page with an assortment of pretty orange embellishments that I just loved.

Honestly *by Elsie Flannigan* **Supplies** *Cardstock:* Bazzill Basics Paper; *Acrylic paint:* Making Memories; *Enamel pieces:* Karen Foster Design; *Ribbon:* C.M. Offray & Son and May Arts; *Brads:* MOD, American Crafts; *Flowers:* Prima; *Pen:* Pigma Micron, Sakura; *Rub-ons:* K&Company.

REAL JOURNALING

My journaling shares how lucky I feel to be part of the Flannigan family. Note how I used specific words to paint a picture of the Flannigan men: adorable, charming, super sweet.

REAL PHOTOGRAPHS

I love this picture of my father-in-law, Tom, wearing his cowboy hat and sunglasses. That great Flannigan smile is just him (and notice how the angle of this photograph captures his handsome profile!).

REAL DESIGN

I wanted to create a sense of harmony that would provide a sense of peace as you enjoy the page. I accomplished this by repeating several different types of lines (hemp rope, rub-ons, ribbon, stitching and title strips) within a very balanced layout.

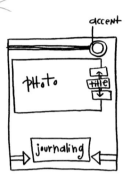

A quick sketch to show my plan!

The Flannigan Charm *by Elsie Flannigan.* **Supplies** *Cardstock:* Bazzill Basics Paper; *Rub-ons:* KI Memories and Dee's Designs; *Photo corners and tape:* Heidi Swapp for Advantus; *Letter tabs:* Autumn Leaves; *Pens:* Uni-ball, Sanford; and Sakura; *Other:* Hemp string and ribbon.

REAL JOURNALING

You know those song lyrics that just get to you and maybe even bring tears to your eyes? They may be the perfect way to add emotion to a page. If the lyrics are beautiful and meaningful to you, why not use them?

REAL PHOTOGRAPHS

Look for real and authentic moments to capture on film. They almost always invoke more powerful emotions than a traditionally posed photo.

REAL DESIGN

I wanted this layout to be unbalanced and edgy, to have a cool artistic effect and invoke a strong emotional response. Note how I created this with elements that are unmistakably me: lots of pink flowers, stitching and pretty ribbons.

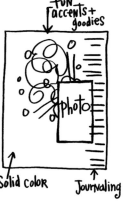

Someday *by Elsie Flannigan.* **Supplies** *Cardstock:* Bazzill Basics Paper; *Patterned papers:* Scenic Route Paper Co. and Chatterbox; *Laser cuts:* Deluxe Designs; *Acrylic paint:* Making Memories; *Flowers:* Prima; *Ribbon:* American Crafts; *Pen:* Uniball; *Other:* Embroidery thread and staples.

REAL JOURNALING

It only takes a few words to remember what was best about being a certain age. I was so lucky to be able to stay home and play with my mom all day!

REAL PHOTOGRAPHS

We all have pictures from our childhood that we might consider "imperfect" because the colors are a little dark or faded. Still, so many things about this photograph are real: my happy smile, the cute floral-print sundress, and the fact that I'm riding my tricycle with no shoes!

REAL DESIGN

Because I love this photograph so much, I wanted to build my page around it. I actually started by centering my picture, then adding embellishments on top of and around it. Note how all of the accents, large and small, are evenly distributed to create a calm, happy, balanced feel.

The Sweet Life *by Elsie Flannigan.* **Supplies** *Cardstock:* Bazzill Basics Paper; *Patterned paper:* Scrapworks; *Stickers:* Doodlebug Design; *Acrylic paint:* Making Memories; *Acetate frame and photo corners:* Heidi Swapp doe Advantus; *Ribbon:* American Crafts; *Pen:* Uni-ball, Sanford; *Other:* Buttons, embroidery thread and rhinestones.

THREE MORE STRATEGIES
Here are three other strategies I use to make sure my layouts are me:

1. **Make sketches.** I always carry my little pink sketchbook in my purse. It doesn't matter where I am—if I see something I love, I'll make a note of it. My sketchbook is packed with topic ideas, unique color combinations and fun ideas for layouts! I use my sketchbook as a starting point to transfer the things I love to my scrapbook pages.

2. **Follow design rules, and bend or break them, too.** I follow, bend or break design rules to convey the feeling, mood and emotion I want to capture. One of my favorite design elements is line, with its ability to lead the eye from one place to another in a layout. I create line in a variety of ways: rows of brads or buttons, journaling strips, ribbons, photo tape and more.

3. **Use supplies I love.** When I create a page, I always use supplies that are beautiful and meaningful to me. When I use items I love, my personality always comes across on the pages. ♥

10

"extra" details

See how I make

my pages

mine

Ever feel like you have a lot of scrapbooking you'd love to do but just can't seem to find the time? I totally get that. Even as a long-time scrapbooker, it's hard to get as much done as I'd like. That's one reason I keep my layouts pretty simple.

Please don't think I put productivity above everything else, however. For me, every layout I create needs a little extra to help it feel complete, to make it "mine." The details I like to add are fast, fun and easy—the perfect way to strike a balance between getting finished and feeling like an artist. Give the following a try!

by Becky Higgins

1 inked edges

How you do it: Simply take an inkpad or inking tool and gently wipe the ink around the edges of your paper.

Why I like this: It's a nice way to define the edges of your paper. It also adds visual depth and interest.

Binkie Girl *by Becky Higgins.* **Supplies** *Patterned paper, felt flowers, brads and rub-ons:* American Crafts; *Font:* CK Regal, "Creative Clips & Fonts for Special Occasions" CD, *Creating Keepsakes; Ink tool:* Around the Block; *Corner rounder:* EK Success.

2 page pebbles as flower centers

How you do it: Place a clear "pebble" sticker directly on patterned paper and cut around the edges. Adhere this to the center of your flower.

Why I like this: Page pebbles are just cool. The handy-dandy clear ones are especially great since you can use virtually any patterned paper under the pebble!

ELEVENTH MONTH

Eleventh Month *by Becky Higgins.* **Supplies** *Cardstock:* Bazzill Basics Paper; *Patterned paper:* Chatterbox; *Letter stickers:* American Crafts; *Flowers, brads and page pebbles:* Making Memories; *Font:* Abadi MT Condensed Light, downloaded from the Internet; *Other:* Thread.

3 sewing

How you do it: Ever stitched a straight line on a sewing machine? That's all this is! Not familiar with a sewing machine? Ask a friend or your mother-in-law or neighbor to show you how easy it really is.

Why I like this: It's quick, subtle and a fantastic way to attach items (especially pockets) to your pages. This technique won't be going out of style any time soon.

4 polaroid-style photos

CONNECTING
ROOTS
IN NORTH CAROLINA

{ JONES FAMILY REUNION • MT. AIRY, NC • JULY 2006 }

Life's Purpose Discover—
The purpose of life is to discover you
mine: that everyone else my age is an adult, whereas
s begun to occur to me that life is a stage I'm go
There is a fountain of youth: It is your mind, y
The way to know life is to love many things.
say that life is a party. You join it after its
lover of life makes the whole world one big family.

a piece of my heart belongs in North Carolina. and it should.
a good part of my heritage is rooted there — my mother's
side of the family, to be exact. The faces shown in the
photographs above are people that I have come to love.
I still have so much to learn about them but I love
my ancestors and honor my past. Going to Mt. airy,
NC with some of my family was an absolute pleasure.
We loaded up in 2 vehicles and drove the six-hour
(ish) drove through the familiar and picturesque
country that I have seen so many times before on
road trips in my life. We would often visit my
Grandma Esther Johnson and others there. and now—
it was a Jones reunion that brought us there this time.
The sweet woman who organized the reunion is
Margaret Akin (B&W photo above) and it is just
uncanny how much she resembles annie Jones,
(shown left of Margaret) who was my grandma's
aunt. and the photo at left of us, is when we visited
my great aunt Virgie (on her 89th birthday).

How you do it: When matting your photos, leave an inch of white at the bottom and only ⅛" around the sides and the top edge.

Why I like this: Reminiscent of old-fashioned Polaroids, this is a fun style for photos and the perfect way to add journaling and captions.

My parents spent HOURS working on a huge pedigree chart for the Jones reunion.

I know my dad loves any opportunity to work on family history stuff so this was fun for him & Mom.

Jonathan & Tina and their 4 kids were part of our group that travelled down from MD, as well as Alyssa & the girls (from London).

I love these guys! Uncle Mel is my Grandma Johnson's youngest brother. He and Aunt Denise barely returned from their mission in Canada.

This is the countryside I love. Absolute perfection. And it's the view from the grave site where my grandparents (Jacob & Esther) are buried.

This home belonged to my gr. grandmother Emma Jones Marion's older brother, Robert Theodore Jones. We loved seeing family homes.

We formed a "Jones Family Choir" and sang in the local ward in church the next day. (The sheet music & church program are behind this page)

along with my grandparents (grave stone shown here with Porter), my gr. grandfather — Jacob L. Johnson Sr. — and his 1st wife are also buried here.

The reunion was held at a park, under a pavillion — very traditional summer family reunion style ☺

Connecting with Our Roots by Becky Higgins. **Supplies** *Patterned paper:* 7gypsies; *Photo corners:* Heidi Swapp for Advantus; *Ribbon:* Prima; *Font:* CK Regal, *"Creative Clips & Fonts for Special Occasions"* CD, Creating Keepsakes.

5 | split fold-back

How you do it: Using a pair of scissors, snip straight into your paper (perpendicular to the edges) as little or as much as you'd like. Fold back the corners (again, a little or a lot—that's up to you). Insert brads in the corners to secure them to the page.

Why I like this: It helps me show off cute, double-sided patterned paper!

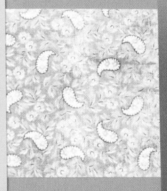

Happy Anniversary by Becky Higgins. **Supplies** Cardstock: Bazzill Basics Paper; Patterned paper: Wild Asparagus, My Mind's Eye; Brads: Doodlebug Design; Font: Clique-Serif, downloaded from the Internet.

6 | colored text

How you do it: In a Word document, highlight the text you want colored. Select Font > Color and double-click on your preferred color choice. Print.

Why I like this: Black text is classic—no doubt—but sometimes you want color to highlight key sections of text.

enlargements

How you do it: I enlarge my photos by digitally cropping them to the size I want (this example is 12" x 3") and placing that image on a "canvas" in Photoshop. The canvas can be any standard-size print. In this case, it's an 8" x 12" canvas. I have that 8" x 12" printed. Since my image doesn't take up the whole print, I cut that part out and it's ready for my page.

Why I like this: Large photos add drama and focus. They give your eye a place to go before viewing the rest of the layout.

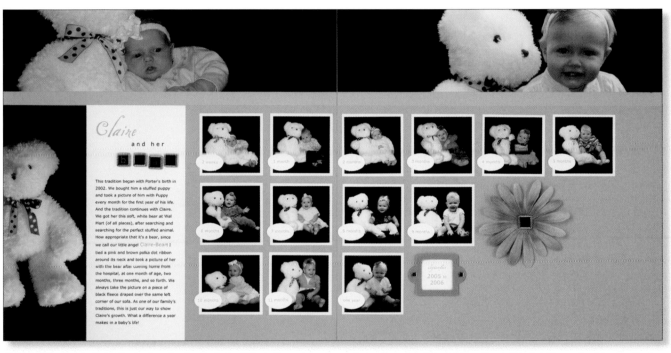

Claire and Her Bear *by Becky Higgins.* **Supplies** *Cardstock:* Bazzill Basics Paper; *Large flower:* Jo-Ann Scrap Essentials; *Chipboard bookplate:* Heidi Swapp for Advantus; *Brads:* Making Memories; *Square letter brads:* Colorbök; *Oval punch:* Emagination Crafts; *Fonts:* CK Elegant (title), "Fresh Fonts" CD, *Creating Keepsakes;* Verdana (journaling), Microsoft Word.

Large photos add drama and focus. Look how compelling simple strips can be.

8 little prints

How you do it: Again, I use Photoshop, but most photo-editing software will do the same trick. I drag-and-drop several photos onto a 4" x 6" printable canvas. I size them to fit, then when I print out the canvas I have a grouping of perfect miniatures.

Why I like this: Little prints help me get more on a page when I want to include a lot but don't want to take up a lot of space in my scrapbook. Now it's easier than ever to cover a whole birthday, weekend getaway or Thanksgiving on one layout. I have a lot of layouts I want to do, so this is important to me. Besides, those little prints are also really cute!

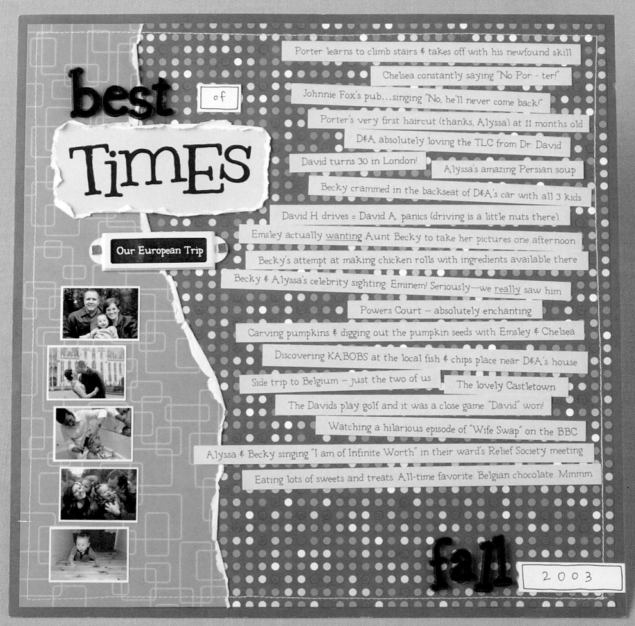

Best of Times *by Becky Higgins.* **Supplies** *Patterned paper and acrylic letters:* KI Memories; *Black letter stickers ("times"):* Doodlebug Design; *Bookplate and brads:* Making Memories; *Font:* CK Typeset, "Creative Clips & Fonts by Becky Higgins" CD, *Creating Keepsakes; Other:* Thread.

photo corners in unexpected places

How you do it: Whether your photo corners are self-adhesive or not, place them on the corners of your photo, journaling block or patterned paper. Or, stick the whole thing to your page.

Why I like this: Paper photo corners provide form and function, and I love that! Of course I use them on my photos a lot (just look at the layouts in this article), but sometimes it's fun to put corners in not-so-expected places, such as the edge of a journaling block or as a frame around a piece of patterned paper.

Brugges Cont. *by Becky Higgins.* **Supplies** *Patterned paper:* Daisy D's Paper Co.; *Photo corners:* 3L Corp. (black) and Canson (tan); *Large bracket:* Printed in Times New Roman on white cardstock, then cut out; *Letter stamps:* Little Black Dress Designs.

10 circle in the title

How you do it: If you have non-sticky letters, lay them out, then decide where you want your punched-out circle to go. Adhere the circle to the page, then glue all the letters down. If you have rub-on letters or stickers, determine where the circle is going before those sticky letters reach the paper. It's not easy to move them should you change your mind.

Why I like this: A bold circle—even if it's not very large—brings emphasis to a title. ♥

Thanksgiving *by Becky Higgins.* **Supplies** *Cardstock:* Bazzill Basics Paper; *Circle punch:* EK Success; *Die-cut letters:* QuicKutz; *Other:* Thread.

4 fun WAYS 2 BREAK the RULES

BY RACHEL THOMAE

TRY SOMETHING NEW TODAY!

Write an article on breaking the rules? Me? I'm not so sure. You see, in high school I was the perfect student—honest. Well, except for those four tardies to typing class that landed me in Saturday morning detention.

So, why the article then? While breaking the rules may have left us in detention in high school, you'll be happy to know that it's A-OK to break the rules in scrapbooking! Honest! Now, you don't have to break the rules with every layout you create . . . but you really should think about it once in a while. Experiment with a digital technique, journal from a new perspective or just have fun goofing around.

Ready to break some scrapbooking rules? Here's the how-to from four CK readers!

I am RECLAIMING my life from breast cancer! I had cancer, it does not have me. I am afraid, but will not live each day in fear. I am not a victim. I am strong and courageous. I am moving on. I am LIVING my life. I am cherishing each day! I am delighting in all the simple things. I am enjoying nature. I am a wife. I am devoted to my family. I am in LOVE with my husband. I am a mother. I am so proud of the man our son is becoming. I am looking forward to what the FUTURE will bring. I am excited to have wrinkles and crow's feet. I am hoping to celebrate many more birthdays. I am so very LUCKY to be 36. I am having fun with scrapbooking again. I am more passionate about recording my life and my loves. I am AWARE of how precious and fleeting life is. I am not going to waste a single moment on anything that does not bring me joy. I am a changed person. I am the 1 in 8. I am the 20 percent. I am more than a statistic. I am a friend. I am INSPIRED to share my creativity. I am going to live my dreams. I am not going to just wait for things to happen. I am going to live the life I've dreamed. I am healing physically. I am healing emotionally. I am loved by so many. I am blessed. I am a SURVIVOR!

I am...

I Am by Dana Hollis Miron. **Supplies** *Cardstock:* Bazzill Basics Paper; *Patterned paper:* K&Company and 7gypsies; *Computer fonts:* Susie's Hand and Perpetua, downloaded from the Internet.

the RULe

A good scrapbook page must feature at least one photograph.

BReaK it!

Dana created a scrapbook page with no photographs at all—but her words tell a compelling story. Says Dana, "This layout is a reminder of what a wonderful life I have. It's also an opportunity to share what I feel in my heart."

HOMEWORK

Create a layout centered around an "I Am" statement.

EXTRA CREDIT

Celebrate the person you've become through your life experiences—journal with a focus on your strengths!

The good...

1. My eyes

2. I am honest and trustworthy

3. I am creative and artsy

4. My photos and albums are organized

5. I have an amazing memory. Dates, places or people, everything.

...the (not so) bad...

1. My moles

2. I am overly anal

3. I am obsessive about scrapbooking

4. I hate doing housework

5. I always take the easiest road in life

2006

...but the ugly.

1. My acne   2. I am whiney

3. I worry to much about getting the picture, that I miss enjoying the moment

4. My car is very messy and dirty

5. I don't shave my legs in winter

The Good, The (Not So) Bad, But the Ugly *by Angela Marvel.* **Supplies** *Cardstock:* Bazzill Basics Paper; *Patterned paper:* Bo-Bunny Press; *Ribbon:* C.M. Offray & Son; *Brads and stamp:* Carolee's Creations; *Computer font:* Garamond, Microsoft Word; *Software:* Adobe Photoshop, Adobe Systems; *Other:* Ribbon, flowers and thread.

the RULe

Photographs work best as squares or rectangles.

BReaK it!

Angela's triangle-shaped photo creates a visual path on her page. Note how your eye is drawn first to her photo, then "reads" through the page from left to right and toward the bottom.

HOMEWORK

Use a template or a computer-editing program to crop a picture into a triangle on your next layout.

EXTRA CREDIT

Angela says, "All of the journaling on my layout is true!" Write about the truths in your life (even if it means admitting your car is messy!).

I didn't know I liked to ride. In fact, I was pretty much opposed to all manner of physical activity until I met Christopher, and his beloved Bianchi. When I saw the amount of time Chris spent out on the road, I figured it was either spend lots of time alone, or learn to love cycling. So I bought a bike and we headed up to the mountains. If you want to find out just how out of **SHARED** shape you really are, this is an excellent way. But with a little time and a lot of effort, I was able to keep up and I actually started to have fun. These days we spend all of our spring and summer weekends in the White Mountains, surrounded by fresh air and beautiful country. We even pull Zoe along behind us. I look forward to the day when she gets her first bicycle, and I hope she'll discover that she loves riding too. **PASSION**

Shared Passion *by Danielle Catalano-Titus.* **Supplies** *Software:* Adobe Photoshop, Adobe Systems; *Digital stamp:* Downloaded from *www.Scrapartist.com*; *Overlay:* Downloaded from *www.SomethingBlueStudios.com*; *Computer fonts:* Trebuchet MS and Plastique, downloaded from the Internet.

the RULe

A square or rectangular presentation is most effective for journaling.

BReaK it!

Take a close look at how Danielle's circle-shaped journaling helps connect it to her photo. The special treatment helps communicate visually how bicycling is a bond that connects her family.

HOMEWORK

Go circular with your journaling . . . or add words in an unexpected place on your layout.

EXTRA CREDIT

Danielle's journaling describes how she was once "pretty much opposed to all manner of physical activity." Create a layout about something you once disliked but now embrace!

santa
barbara in fall
one of the most
lovely places of all
reminds me of spain
where i long to be again
here or there
life is beautiful

la vida es bella

La Vida Es Bella *by Cherie Mask*. **Supplies** *Software:* Adobe Photoshop CS, Adobe Systems; *Digital stitching:* Sew ScrapPEA Birdie Stitches by Rhonna Farrer, downloaded from *www.twopeasinabucket.com*; *Computer fonts:* Stan's Hand and Centaur, downloaded from the Internet.

the RULe

Don't combine elements with contrasting patterns.

BReaK it!

Look how Cherie successfully combines ornamental patterned paper with the spiral pattern in her photo. Although the patterns are contrasting, they support Cherie's message that "Life is beautiful" and reflect how Santa Barbara reminds her of Spain.

HOMEWORK

Go on a field trip and look for unique objects you can scan and add to your layouts as embellishments. (The "patterned paper" in this layout is actually lace that was scanned.)

EXTRA CREDIT

Title a layout with a phrase in a foreign language! ❤

ILLUSTRATION © ADRIAN D'ALIMONTE

10 Ways
to Get in Shape
Savvy ways to use shapes on your layout

Shapes are big in my house right now. My son Simon is all about identifying circles, squares, rectangles and triangles, along with the occasional oval and diamond.

I, too, see shapes everywhere. (Kind of like X-ray vision, but on the outside. A little nutty? Yep!) When looking at everyday objects, I'm often drawn to the overall shape. Rather than a tree, I see a triangle. Rather than a car, I see a rectangle or square.

BY ALI EDWARDS

In scrapbooking, geometric shapes dominate the landscape. Photos, accents and journaling blocks most often appear as rectangles, squares and circles. Playing with shapes feels like putting together puzzle pieces, mixing and matching until each element finds its own special home.

Here's what shapes can do for your page design:

• **ORGANIZE.** Keep things in order and aid in overall flow.

• **ACCESSORIZE.** Make perfect little accents.

• **SYMBOLIZE.** Imply additional meaning.

• **EMPHASIZE.** Highlight particular elements within the overall design.

One of the most effective ways to use shapes is through repetition. Pick one shape and run with it. Let's take a look at what shapes can do for you.

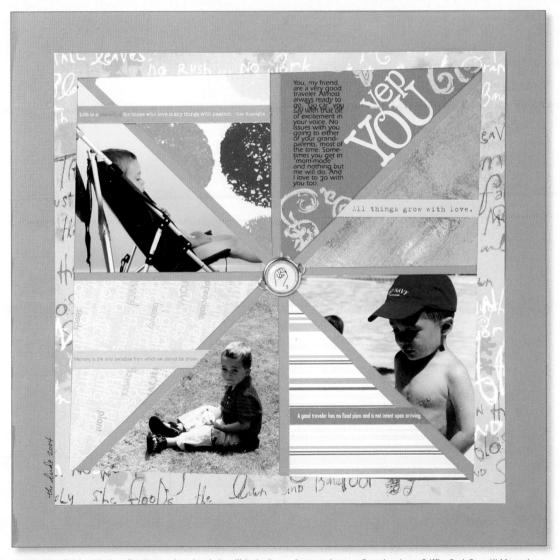

Yep You *by Ali Edwards.* **Supplies** *Textured cardstock:* Bazzill Basics Paper; *Patterned papers:* 7gypsies, Anna Griffin, BasicGrey, KI Memories and Li'l Davis Designs; *Rub-ons and die-cut quotes:* KI Memories; *Circle accents:* K&Company (sign language) and Nunn Design (metal); *Computer font:* Eurostile, Adobe Systems.

Safari *by Ali Edwards.* **Supplies** *Letter stickers:* Gin-X, Imagination Project; *Rub-ons:* Arctic Frog, Fontwerks, KI Memories and Making Memories; *Ribbon:* Scrapworks; *Page protectors:* Pulp.

Organize

Geometric shapes organize the contents of your layout and provide a foundation or structure for your page elements.

1 BUILD A RECTANGULAR FOUNDATION FROM A PHOTO COLLAGE. Notice how two 12"x 12" pages come together to create a rectangle in "Safari" above?

For this layout, simply gather twelve 4" x 6" pictures for a well-composed geometric design. Attach a 6" x 6" page protector to place on top of each page with ribbon for additional photos and titles. Flip up the page protectors to see hidden journaling behind the photos. A great way to connect the two pages visually is to place a rub-on directly onto the seam. Use a craft knife to cut the rub-on right down the middle.

2 CREATE A PAGE WHERE YOU BEGIN BY FOCUSING ON A PARTICULAR SHAPE. Notice how the triangles in my "Yep You" page on page 121 help organize my content: each triangle acts as a home for a photo, quote or journaling.

To keep all the triangles contained, use a craft knife to cut a frame from a sheet of patterned paper. Add a circle accent where each of the triangle points meet for a great finishing touch. On your next layout, play around a bit and substitute two triangles for a square element.

he said
random love
'Your hair looks nice like that.'
'I never want to move out.'
'You have beautiful eyes.'
'Kira dnd Cameron are my best friends.'
'You look cute like that.'
'I like you and Daddy.'
'But your bed is cozier.'
'I always want to be part of the family.'
c
Besides snugs and kisses, this is my favorite kind of love you give us. Random love. The out-of-the-blue sayings that get us right in the heart. The little sentences that are full of meaning. We completely adore you.

Random Love *by Jamie Waters.* **Supplies** *Patterned paper:* American Crafts; *Ribbon:* Scrapworks; *Wood frame, acrylic letters, epoxy letters, chipboard letter and stickers:* Li'l Davis Designs; *Fabric tag:* 7gypsies.

3 IMPLY A SHAPE WITHIN A GATHERING OF SQUARES.

For example, notice how the squares on Jamie's page above are grouped to form one large rectangle.

Add interest to a foundation of six squares by placing your right-justified journaling in one square, creating a collage of accents in another and patterned paper in the third. These make wonderful companions to those three darling photos!

Bloom *by Jamie Waters.* **Supplies** *Patterned papers:* American Crafts, Autumn Leaves, Chatterbox, KI Memories, Making Memories, Paperfever and Scrapworks; *Rub-ons:* 7gypsies (arrow), Autumn Leaves (stitching) and KI Memories (letters); *Sticker tab:* SEI; *Pen:* American Crafts.

Accessorize

Geometric shapes make excellent "accessories" for layouts.

1 PIECE BASIC SHAPES TOGETHER TO CREATE FUN AND FUNKY ACCENTS. Take a look at the cool flowers on Jamie's page made from triangles of patterned paper. In addition, notice how the overall shape of each flower is a circle, creating a nice contrast with the rectangle photo on the top. An easy way to create small triangles is to use a square punch and then cut the squares in half. Voila!

Little Things by Ali Edwards. **Supplies** *Textured cardstock:* Bazzill Basics Paper; *Patterned papers:* Autumn Leaves, Chatterbox and Li'l Davis Designs (circles); *Label stickers:* Dymo; *Large circle stamp:* Fontwerks; *Stamping ink:* ColorBox Fluid Chalk, Clearsnap; *Pen:* American Crafts; *Computer font:* 2Peas Sunflower, downloaded from *www.twopeasinabucket.com.*

2 USE GEOMETRIC SHAPES TO SIMPLY AND BEAUTIFULLY DRESS UP A LAYOUT. Combine basic shapes from different mediums to create a smart look.

On this layout, I've combined circles cut from patterned paper with large circle stamps. Also notice the combination of patterned-paper rectangles and squares that create the background foundation.

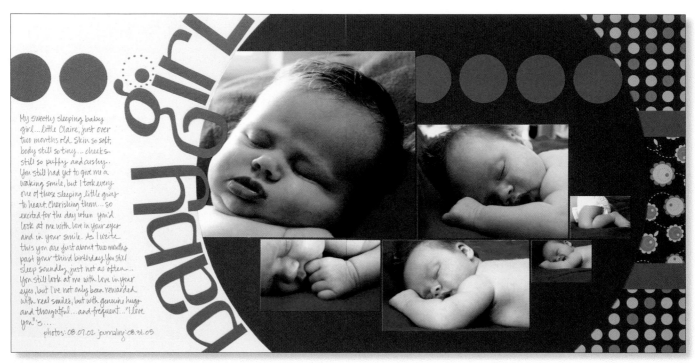

My sweetly sleeping baby girl… little Claire, just over two months old. Skin so soft, body still so tiny… cheeks still so puffy and cushy… You still had yet to give me a waking smile, but I took every one of those sleeping little grins to heart. Cherishing them… so excited for the day when you'd look at me with love in your eyes and in your smile. As I write this yr are just about two months past your third birthday. You still sleep soundly, just not as often… You still look at me with love in your eyes, but I've not only been rewarded with real smiles, but with genuine hugs and thoughtful… and frequent… "I love you"'s…

photos: 08.07.02 journaling: 08.31.05

Baby Girl *by Carrie Owens.* **Supplies** *Textured cardstock:* Bazzill Basics Paper; *Patterned paper:* Die Cuts With a View; *Pen:* Zig Writer, EK Success; *Title font:* Carrie's own design.

Symbolize

Geometric shapes can be used to symbolize additional meaning, both literally and figuratively. Jacci Howard Bear for www.about.com suggests that certain shapes symbolize the following:

- **CIRCLE:** Infinity, protective, well-rounded, complete, secure
- **SQUARE AND RECTANGLE:** Honesty, stability, equality, rigidity
- **TRIANGLE:** Action, conflict, growth, direction

1 **USE CIRCLE SHAPES TO CONVEY AND SYMBOLIZE A SENSE OF CARE AND PROTECTION.** I especially love Carrie's repetition of circles and the warm color combination that fits wonderfully with the theme.

3 by Ali Edwards. **Supplies** *Textured cardstock:* Bazzill Basics Paper; *Patterned papers:* Anna Griffin, BasicGrey and KI Memories; *Definition accents:* Wild Asparagus, My Mind's Eye; *Stamping ink:* StazOn, Tsukineko; *Metal "3" and "S" (used to resist stamp):* KI Memories; *Pen:* American Crafts.

2 TAKE ADVANTAGE OF THE STRONG DIRECTIONAL POWER OF TRIANGLES. They move the eye inward, *just like an arrow,* toward the center of the layout you've created.

Another idea: Rather than placing your journaling alongside your photo, slice your photo about a third of the way from the edge. Place your journaling in a rectangular block between the two sections of the photo.

Look Up *by Danielle Thompson.* **Supplies** *Rub-ons:* Doodlebug Design; *Buttons:* Bazzill Basics Paper and foof-a-La, *Embroidery floss:* DMC; *Ribbon:* Michaels; *Fabric fasteners:* 7gypsies; *Mini-brads:* Making Memories; *Pens:* EK Success and Sanford.

Emphasize

Shapes can be used to aid in movement and focus, directing your eye right to the heart of the layout.

1 **DIRECT THE VIEWER'S EYES THROUGH THE LAYOUT.** On Danielle's page, the triangular shape of the photo in the lower center of the layout leads your eye back up to the photo in the upper left corner. Danielle used strong diagonal lines in her page design to lend a feeling of upward motion to the page she created.

By the Lake *by Ali Edwards.* **Supplies** *Textured cardstock:* Bazzill Basics Paper; *Patterned paper:* Fontwerks; *Circle accents:* KI Memories and SEI; *Rub-ons:* KI Memories (letters) and Autumn Leaves (stitching); *Letter stickers and pen:* American Crafts.

2 DRAW ATTENTION TO A PAR-TICULAR ELEMENT. To emphasize the photo of Ruby's back, I changed it to black and white and cropped it into a circle.

To balance the layout I added two circle accents and used white type for the title. This was easy and effective!

The Bond *by Carrie Owens.* **Supplies** *Textured cardstock:* Bazzill Basics Paper; *Chipboard letters:* Li'l Davis Designs; *Pen:* Zig Writer, EK Success.

3 USE A SHAPE TO GUIDE THE VIEWER'S EYE TO YOUR FOCAL POINT. On Carrie's page, your eye follows the movement of the rectangle photos from one side of the layout to the other, resting on the large photo at right. Carrie also employs rectangular chipboard accents to aid in the overall repetition of shape. ♥

i ♥ hearts

Fall in love—with seven easy heart techniques I couldn't resist! Whether you're doodling, cutting or drawing, you'll create terrific, top-notch looks in record time. You've gotta love that!

∧ **You'll love this technique!**
Cut a heart freehand from cardstock, then trim the inside to create a frame. Simple yet oh-so-cool. ＞

Looks Like Love *by Vanessa Hudson.* **Supplies** *Cardstock:* Die Cuts With a View; *Patterned papers:* BasicGrey; *Paper-sack paper:* Big Art; *Flower stamp:* Technique Tuesday; *Pens:* Zig Writer (black), EK Success; Uni-ball Signo (white), Sanford; *Buttons:* Junkitz; *Tab die cut:* Sizzix; *Colored pencils:* Prismacolor, Sanford; *Other:* Buttons and thread.

I ♥ how Pam made use of the heart cards from an incomplete deck.

<< **You'll love this technique!**

Pencil in a heart on your layout, then stitch over it! Notice how this heart perfectly frames the heads of its two main subjects.

I Love My Dog *by Pam Callaghan.* **Supplies** *Cardstock:* Bazzill Basics Paper; *Stamping ink:* Ranger Industries; *Rickrack and stickers:* Making Memories; *Font:* 2Peas Old Type, *www.twopeasinabucket.com; Other:* Cards and thread.

> **You'll love this technique!**

Cut thin strips from cardstock and patterned paper, then form them into a heart. Add word strips for your journaling and stitch over the heart to complete.

The Contents of My Heart *by Melissa Kelley.* **Supplies** *Cardstock:* Bazzill Basics Paper; *Patterned papers and letter stickers:* Scrapworks; *Vellum:* DMD, Inc.; *Rub-ons:* Heidi Swapp for Advantus (flourish), Scrapworks (small hearts) and Making Memories (black letters); *Chipboard letters:* Making Memories ("e") and Heidi Swapp for Advantus (all others); *Paint:* Plaid Enterprises; *Fonts:* Susie's Hand, Miss and Jane Austen, downloaded from the Internet; 2Peas Wedding Day, *www.two-peasinabucket.com.*

I ♥ how Melissa used photo size to represent the proportional importance of each object.

I ♥ how Sharon stitched on her chipboard, using a heavy needle on thin chipboard sheets.

My Heart Throb *by Sharon Laakkonen.* **Supplies** *Cardstock:* WorldWin; *Patterned papers, rub-ons and coaster hearts:* Gin-X, Imagination Project; *Stamping ink:* Ranger Industries; *Pen:* Sharpie, Sanford; *Other:* Thread.

∧ You'll love this technique!

Chipboard hearts are hip, but hand-cut chipboard outlines are even better! Simply cut around the leftover "negative" sheet of chipboard hearts, then add the cutout shape around the precut hearts. Top them with coordinating patterned papers.

5 more heart techniques

Want other ideas to use on your pages? Try these!

• Pull out your decorative scissors and cut hearts with extra flair around the edges.

• Ink heart stickers (before removing them from the sheet) for customized colors.

• Print heart dingbats on cardstock to create a border.

• Replace "o" letters in your journaling with doodled hearts. You can even replace "a" letters—just attach a line to the right side.

• Photograph hands formed into a heart shape and include the picture on your page.

I ♥ the nontraditional color combination on this page!

< You'll love this technique!

Cut hearts from felt, then layer for added appeal. Draw freehand, trace from stencils, or print hearts from your computer and use them as patterns.

Still with You *by Corinne Delis.* **Supplies** *Cardstock:* Bazzill Basics Paper; *Patterned paper, chipboard shape and chipboard letters:* cherryArte; *Font:* Arial, Microsoft Word; *Other:* Felt.

> You'll love this technique!

Paint freestyle hearts with watercolor! Experiment on small squares that you can add to your layout. If you don't like how one turns out, you won't have to redo the entire layout. Love that!

Our Valentine Philosophy *by Wilna Furstenberg.* **Supplies** *Cardstock;* Bazzill Basics Paper; *Stamp ("Copyright"):* 7gypsies; *Stamping ink:* Memories, Stewart Superior Corporation; *Watercolor and watercolor paper:* Winsor and Newton; *Pen:* Pigment Inker, Staedtler; *Other:* Thread.

I ♥ Wilna's journaling and her Valentine philosophy!

{simply you} ♥

548112210[5414]*51001516541218843789181304103217 4 (1452156)/4516316*4115487

Quite honestly, I finished this page days before I could figure out what to put in the journaling. It sat on my desk waiting for the words to come. I guess you could say I was intimidated if you will by these awesome pictures. Something about them captured my heart. I stared at them over and over, each time completely in awe of your beauty. You my child are so incredibly adorable. From that hat which is a favorite of mine (you own two!) with those luscious curls peeking out from below it. Your sparkly eyes draw me in each time. I could just look at these pictures over and over again. I look at them and I feel so much in my heart for you. So much in fact that I can't put it into words. I can't articulate the deepness of my love for you. Not a day goes by that I don't feel so incredibly lucky to be your mom. You are the light of my life... that is certain. There is no place on earth I would rather be than with you. We have fun together. We mesh well. We have a little routine that is all our own. Truth be told, not all moments in our life are filled with bliss. We have our

share of ups and downs. But my personal saving grace is our love amidst the chaos. For me, the house could be falling apart and your little brown eyes in front of me ask to play trains (again) and I willingly do it. The bond we share is irreplaceable. I have something that every mom is not lucky enough to have with her child. This is why I chose to not work; this is why I stay home. For the love... so yeah, our life is chaotic at best, but it is worth every minute. EVERY SINGLE temper tantrum, every whine, every toss, every spit, and every spilled juice. It is all worth it; because I have you little man to look up at me and say, "Mommy, I love you." Those words are more powerful than any negative aspect of life. And the pure sound of them makes me want to drop to my knees and thank God that I am so lucky to have you as my child. So why is it that I have a hard time saying what I feel? Why is it that my heart skips a beat and I have to catch my breath when I look at these photos. Well quite simply put...it is because of you. You are simply too amazing!

Simply You *by Candace Leonard.* **Supplies** *Cardstock:* BasicGrey; *Patterned papers:* KI Memories (stripe and text) and FontWerks (dot); *Rub-ons:* KI Memories (white numbers), foof-a-La for Autumn Leaves (brackets) and Heidi Swapp for Advantus (stars); *Chipboard letters:* Heidi Swapp for Advantus; *Acrylic letters, circle accent and ribbon:* KI Memories; *Font:* AL Worn Machine, *www.twopeasinabucket.com;* *Other:* Thread and transparency.

You'll love this technique!

This ribbon heart is subtle, yet cool. To make it, start by sketching a heart in pencil, then tack down the bottom "v" shape with a stitch on the ribbon. Next, fold the upper "v" section and stitch, then finish up with the two top sides. ♥

Send Us Your Work
Do you have scrapping solutions or layout ideas for each season? Send us your work! You'll find current calls and submission information online at *www.creatingkeepsakes.com/mag/your_work*.

your style:
discovering your personal color palette

When someone asks, "What's your favorite color?" it's probably a fairly easy question to answer. However, determining a favorite color palette—groups of colors that work together—can be a bit trickier. Hit the locations below to discover which personal color palettes you can transfer to your scrapbooking style.

ASSIGNMENT 1:

Your Make-Up Drawer. Okay, it may be neat or it may be a complete mess, but your make-up drawer is a great place to discover colors that already work for you. Start with your lipstick. Do you like bright true colors, such as true reds, or do you favor lighter pastel shades with just a hint of color? Now look at your eye shadow. Do you prefer buying an eye color set that includes three or four different coordinating shades, or do you prefer to pick out single shades that you know will work well together? Think about the colors. Do you stick with the "tried and true," or do you like to experiment with trendy colors? Do you prefer matte-finish products, or do you have any glittery products? Can you make a jump from the colors you like to wear to the colors you like to scrap? ♥

ASSIGNMENT 2:

The Jewelry Counter. Go to a store that sells a variety of jewelry and look at the necklaces. If you could buy three necklaces, which three would you buy? Do you like the classic pendant necklaces with a single stone hanging from a delicate chain? (Perhaps you like classical colors and clean lines on your layouts.) Do you like hand-painted beads strung together in an interesting array of sizes and colors? (Perhaps you'd like to try those colors on a scrapbook page.)

ASSIGNMENT 3:

The Paint Chip Aisle. Go to your favorite hardware store and stand in front of the paint chips. This time, don't worry about which colors will work best on your next layout. Stand there and look at the paint chips and then choose the three colors that appeal to you the most. Pull them out and put them next to each other. Think about why you like those three colors. Do you like them together as much as you like them separately? Would you like to scrapbook with those colors?

Question:

What's your favorite color? Where would we find it in your home?

Kelly Anderson: "I love red, especially red shoes! My passion for the color red is most evident in my closet!"

Lilac Chang: "I love purple. It's fresh and bold, whether it's on my couch or in my garden."

Brenda Arnall: "I love aqua and turquoise colors in my home. Even my dishes are aqua. However, I'll admit—I do have a hard time scrapbooking with this color!"

Karen Russell: "My favorite color is red! I love red as an accent color. I love red shoes, red candles and my red beaded throw that goes across the bottom of my bed."

Karen Burniston: "My favorite color is blue, and you'll find it all over my house. I've got a comfy blue chair, blue accent couch pillows, a favorite pair of blue jeans and a two-foot stack of blue cardstock!"

Shannon Wolz: "My favorite colors switch constantly. Right now, I like chocolate brown, Caribbean blue, pale pink and olive green. My house is decorated with lots of greens, but my clothing is usually pastel or bright."

the emotional life of
COLOR

Express how you feel without saying a word

Sitting on my floor with a pile of photos in my lap, I thumb through my cardstock. I'm about to "feel" my way through the color selection process. Hmmm, that lavender is soft, even a bit whimsical. Might work. Definitely not the charcoal—too formal. Navy blue feels cold and impersonal with these photos. Lavender it is, then. How do you decide which colors to emphasize on a layout? While you may not always be aware of it, color influences more than just the eye. It impacts your emotions as well! In fact, when selecting a color to frame your memories, how that color makes you "feel" may just be the most important consideration of all.

by Sharon Stasney

Color Chart

The following color chart highlights the physical and emotional effects of color. Use the chart—and your own feelings—to make your color selection a matter of heart and mind.

Red

Known for energy in China and courage in the United States, red is sexy, passionate, fiery and bold. Physically it increases your heart rate and your adrenaline. This is not a thinking color—it's about taking action.

Pastels/White

The soft, floating look of pastels enhances feelings of purity, cleanliness, innocence and tenderness. Pastels also encourage the mind to wander, allowing for a creative, playful experience. Pure white is associated with precision, inclusiveness, fairness and spirituality.

Orange

The color for clowns and cheerfulness, orange is stimulating. Known to physically activate the lower half of the body, orange represents change—stirring things up—and playfulness. Orange is associated with "joy" more than any other color.

Neutrals/Black

The softer side of nature's palette, neutrals feel earthy, comforting, solid and grounding. They increase feelings of stability, protection and reliability. Deeper neutrals, leading into black, can also feel sophisticated, dramatic and powerful.

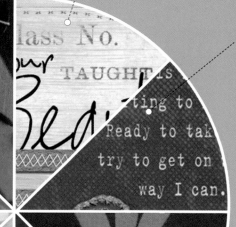

Purple

While lavender captures the angelic nature of children, purple in general stimulates brain activity more than any other color! (Try staring at something purple before you leave to take a test.) Associated with royalty, enlightenment and wisdom, purple will open you to higher realms of awareness.

Yellow

Associated with the life-sustaining force of the sun, yellow offers a wide range of benefits. It's been shown to increase self-confidence (especially in younger children), optimism and feelings of personal power. Physically, yellow boosts gastric juices, which helps release fears and phobias.

Green

Everywhere in nature, green represents balancing metabolic processes as well as emotions. Associated with a variety of symbols (growth, money, luck, freshness and health), green equals goodness.

Blue

Ahh, the soothing effects of blue. Blue represents loyalty, honesty, tranquility and peace. Too much blue (and too dark) can feel somber, however. Blue slows the respiratory system, stabilizes an erratic heart rate and balances the thyroid, so go blue to enhance inner calm.

A COLOR FOR EVERY MOOD

We selected the following layouts to illustrate the emotional impact of color. Each scrapbooker let the "feeling" in her photo influence her color selection. We think you'll love the results!

Lively Yellow

A burst of energy flows through this layout. With such sunny, uplifting colors, it's not difficult to see why yellow raises feelings of self-esteem in children.

My Wink *by Diana Lyn C. McGraw.* **Supplies** *Cardstock:* Bazzill Basics Paper; *Patterned papers:* KI Memories and Bazzill Basics Paper; *Flower punch:* EK Success; *Title letters:* Paper Studio ("my") and Heidi Swapp for Advantus ("wink"); *Rub-ons:* Die Cuts With a View; *Gems:* The Beadery; *Other:* Patterned flowers.

Exuberant Orange

The joy in this boy's face comes to life when framed with playful, cheerful orange.

Zany *by Sharon Laakkonen.* **Supplies** *Cardstock:* Bazzill Basics Paper; *Patterned papers:* SEI and Scrapworks; *Wood letter:* Li'l Davis Designs; *Stickers:* 7gypsies; *Large rickrack:* May Arts; *Pen:* Zig Millennium, EK Success; *Other:* Thread.

Cheeky Red

Passion is a given when lovebirds are wrapped in
red's stirring embrace.

Love Birds *by Danielle Thompson.* **Supplies** *Cardstock:* Die Cuts With a View; *Transparencies and staples:* Office Depot; *Felt:* Jo-Ann Scrap Essentials; *Embroidery floss:* DMC; *White pen:* Uni-ball, Sanford; *Bird die cut:* Sassafras Lass; *Letter stamps:* FontWerks; *Stamping ink:* VersaColor, Tsukineko; *Markers:* American Crafts.

Generous Green

The health, growth and goodness of green are perfect complements to the energetic grin of this growing boy.

My, How You've Grown by Staci McFadden. **Supplies** *Background*: Sausan Designs, *www.scrapbookgraphics.com*; *Striped paper*: Kim Christensen's "RAD Refresh" kit, *www.scrapartist.com*; *Green clip*: Gina Cabrera's "Summer Essentials," *www.digitaldesignessentials.com*; *File tab and measuring tape*: Katie Pertiet, *www.designerdigitals.com*; *Stamped letters*: Michelle Coleman, *www.scrapartist.com*; *Stitches*: Michelle Coleman's "Boho Chic" kit, *www.scrapartist.com*; *Word strips*: Manda Bean's "Shabby Candy Wrapper," *www.sweetshoppedesigns.com*; *Font*: Elephant, downloaded from the Internet.

Calming Blue

Here, blue's loyalty and honesty provide the perfect
backdrop to a father's day out with his boys.

Amazing Man by Kendra McKracken. **Supplies** *Patterned paper:* BasicGrey; *Hanger:* Junkitz; *Pillow chip:* Autumn Leaves; *Rub-on letters:* Making Memories and Heidi Swapp for Advantus; *Wire heart:* Making Memories; *Acetate overlay:* Hambly Studios; *Stamping ink:* Archival Ink, Ranger Industries; *Ribbon:* Li'l Davis Designs; *Embroidery floss:* DMC; *Font:* Adler, downloaded from www.dafont.com; *Other:* Fabric, twill, star rhinestones, thread, vintage buttons, denim, label and graph paper.

Delightful Purple

Framed in lavender and violet, this layout captures the sacredness of everyday acts, such as eating breakfast in the highchair.

adore

25 months

What is my girl thinking?
You were so very tired.
You just sat so STILL
Being very cooperative when
mommy grabbed her camera
as you sat and just looked at me
for the longest time.

Still *by Joy Bollinger.* **Supplies** *Cardstock*: Bazzill Basics Paper and WorldWin; *Patterned papers and alpha dot stickers on flowers*: Scrapworks; *Photo corners*: Canson; *Rub-ons ("25 months")*: Visu-Com; *Journaling transparency*: Hammermill; *Fonts*: Centabel Book and Poor Richard, downloaded from the Internet; *Flower*: Handmade.

Uplifting Pastels

The childlike playfulness in this photo blooms when
adorned with soft pastels.

Timeless Beauty *by C.D. Muckosky.* **Supplies** *Background paper, striped colors, tie fasteners, catalogued alpha, mini tag and green tags:* Katie Pertiet, www.designerdigitals.com; *Digital library card, photo prongs & red flower, pink painted flower and hemp:* Jackie Eckles, www.designerdigitals.com; *Digital crochet leaf, felt trims, "e" monogram, and slide:* Gina Cabrera, www.digitaldesignessentials.com; *Digital messy stitches:* Holly McCaig, www.plaindigital-wrapper.com; *Software:* Adobe Photoshop CS2, Adobe Systems; *Font:* Tia Bennett collection, Autumn Leaves; *Pen:* Zig Millennium, EK Success; *Watercolor pencils:* Prang; *Photo corners:* Canson; *Other:* Silk flowers.

Quiet Neutrals

To capture her recent experience of widowhood, Stacy McFadden
chose the grounding comfort of brown for most of her layout.
The pink butterfly represents the stirring to life of new hope.

This path isn't one that I chose. It's not one
that I ever thought I would have to take, yet
here I am. I don't like this path but I must
travel it until the road begins to lead to
whatever it is that is next for me. The past
six months have been the hardest of my life.
All of a sudden I'm a widow. A single mom. And
alone. The future is full of uncertainty but I
am finally starting to feel that I am ready to
embrace it. Ready to take a baby step out and
try to get on with life in whatever
way I can.
     I pray for strength to get
     through whatever lies
     ahead. I pray for courage to
     stand tall in the face of
uncertainty. And I pray for wisdom
to help me make the best choices
for myself and my sons.

Moving Forward *by Stacy McFadden.* **Supplies** *Digital background, butterfly, leather trim, metal clip, lace trim and brush strokes:* Gypsy Rose kit by Michelle Coleman, *www.scrapartist.com; Digital photo corner:* Nancie Rowe Janitz' "Quiet Love" kit, *www.scrapartist.com; Digital gingham ribbons and brown stitches:* Katie Pertiet, *www.designerdigitals.com; Digital swirl brushes:* Rhonna Farrer, *www.twopeasinabucket.com; Fonts:* Typical Writer and Texas Hero, *www.dafont.com.*

Daring **Black**

Black layouts are never boring, and the dramatic sophistication of the deep background catapults this layout right into the fascinating zone (just where a young lady wants to be). ♥

Breanna, i love your beautiful blue eyes... they look like jewels to me... you are priceless to me... and to God!

my jewel

My Jewel by Sharon Laakkonen. **Supplies** *Cardstock:* Bazzill Basics Paper; *Patterned paper:* Mara-Mi; *Gems:* Heidi Swapp for Advantus; *Letter mini brads:* Queen & Co.; *Acrylic flowers:* KI Memories; *Pen:* Galaxy Marker, American Craft; *Other:* Thread.

20 quick and easy tips for
filling your pages with color

Bright
and Beautiful
DESIGNS

As soon as the weather warms each year, I'm thrilled to pull out my summer wardrobe. Coral shirts, lime belts, pink Capri pants—it's heaven in my closet after months of winter sweaters. Bright summer colors are just so invigorating! They never fail to inspire.

I love using these exciting colors in my scrapbooks, too! There's just one drawback—sometimes it takes time to find a good balance with so much color. I'm tempted to change my photos to black and white just to simplify the process (especially when I've just picked up a yummy patterned paper at the store and can't wait to use it).

Ever felt the same way? You don't have to any more! Just check out the doable tips on the following pages—you have 20 to choose from on your next summer layout. I've tried them, and they've helped me scrapbook my bright summer pages faster. I'm going to use the extra time to go find a new summer tee!

by Brittany Beattie

tip Overwhelmed by a paper but love the pattern? Cut out and use itas accent instead—that's what Greta did with the flowers on this page.

tip If you're placing bright papers or embellishments near a photo, extend the photo mat to keep the focus on your picture.

tip Include small accents in corners with negative space to add balance.

Summer would not be summer if we didn't visit as many parks and swing sets as humanly possible. Whether an intended destination or one that we just happen upon, finding a swing always brings a smile to your face. However, it is not just a ride on a swing that makes you happy. The "swing song" must also be part of the process.
   "How do you like to go up in a swing? Up in the air so blue. Oh, I do think it is a pleasantest thing, ever a child can do!"
As I push you higher and higher, the song gets louder and louder. Over and over again. So many times that I have tired of it long before you are ready to quit. But seeing you grin from ear to ear and eventually belt out the tune with me, is more than enough encouragement to keep me singing, time and time again.

The Swing Song *by Greta Hammond.* **Supplies** *Textured cardstock:* Bazzill Basics Paper; *Patterned papers:* me & my BIG ideas (flowers) and Doodlebug Design; *Rub-ons:* Making Memories (letters) and Scribbles, Autumn Leaves (ornamental accents); *Flowers:* Doodlebug Design; *Chipboard letters:* Heidi Swapp for Advantus; *Computer font:* Times New Roman, Microsoft Word; *White pen:* Sharpie, Sanford.

tip Work with your photos to create a page design with a natural flow. Here, the blue from the boy's hat inspired the top of the layout, while his green shirt below it inspired the bottom section. The orange circles (arranged in a visual triangle on the pages) mimic the snow cone—the subject of the page.

tip Select a color scheme with only 2–3 colors so it doesn't become overwhelming.

Snowcone *by Bonnie Lotz.* **Supplies** *Patterned papers:* Scenic Route; *Rub-ons:* Making Memories ("Summer") and Doodlebug Design ("Sweet," letter and stitching); *Ribbon:* Making Memories (orange and orange dot) and Close To My Heart (orange gingham); *Ribbon brad:* Memories; *White button:* Making Memories; *Lettering template:* Pebbles Inc. ("Sun"); *Computer font:* CK Newsprint, "Fresh Fonts" CD, *Creating Keepsakes.*

Celebrity Q&A

Q I want to use a bright color scheme on my layout. How do I know which colors to use?

A Look at the colors in your photos. Because most of us wear bright colors during the summer, many of the photos taken then will naturally offer a good starting place for including these hot colors on a layout.

—Lisa Bearnson

tip If you're using bright papers with busy patterns, include blocks of solid-colored cardstock for balance.

tip If you like a pattern in a specific paper but it's set against a neutral color, cut around it and back it with brighter papers, like the oval chain patterns Miley laid over bright-pink cardstock.

tip If you feel like the bright products dominate your photos, don't be afraid to sand the edges. You'll still see the summery colors, but the look won't be as overwhelming.

It was only the first week of summer, and we were going through popsicles like crazy. Who was sneaking them out of the house? I couldn't figure it out, until I caught the pair red handed. Or should I say, sticky orange handed. He's hot mom, he needs a treat, too! It was true...it was crazy hot, and even the dog was smart enough to know that a popsicle hits the spot. So yeah, this was the summer our popsicle bill was huge, but the girl AND the dog couldn't have been happier.

Pupsicle Treat by Miley Johnson. **Supplies** *Textured cardstock:* Bazzill Basics Paper; *Patterned papers:* BasicGrey (pink solid and orange dot), A2Z Essentials (orange floral) and We R Memory Keepers (oval chain pattern); *Letter stickers:* Junkitz; *Chipboard:* We R Memory Keepers (letters) and Technique Tuesday (circle frame); *Fun foam flowers:* Michaels; *Computer fonts:* AL Uncle Charles, downloaded from *www.twopeasinabucket.com*.

Celebrity Q&A

Q I love bright colors but am afraid to venture out and use them on my pages. Any "baby step" tricks I can use?

A Try a tone-on-tone color combo, where you're working with only one bright color variation. Then, on the next page, try adding an additional complementary color. Another tip? Look for color combos that you like in magazines or catalogs and mimic them!

—Heidi Swapp

tip When bright colors fill the center of your page, use small accents near the outer edges to add balance. Courtney used embroidered stitches for the perfect—and especially fun—touch.

tip Help photos "pop" against colorful patterns by matting them on white cardstock.

Summer *by Courtney Walsh.* **Supplies** *Kraft cardstock:* Hobby Lobby; *Patterned papers:* Scrapworks; *Rub-ons:* Autumn Leaves ("in," "o," "g" and "i"), Creative Imaginations ("G" and "S"); *Brads:* Making Memories; *Flowers:* Prima; *Letter stickers:* American Crafts (black and white), KI Memories (white "s" and "n") and Chatterbox ("N"); *Embroidery floss:* DMC; *Pen:* Uni-ball Signo, Sanford.

Celebrity Q&A

Q When working with bright-colored patterns, when should you stick with a monochromatic scheme versus one with several colors?

A I try to save my busy, bright paper for layouts that include only one or two enlarged photos. They carry enough visual weight that they don't compete with the paper. I save the monochromatic schemes for layouts with several smaller photos that contain lots of different colors.

—Erin Lincoln

tip Use neutral colors, like white or black, for your page background. Not only will it give your eye a place to rest, it will also help the bright elements "pop" visually on your page.

tip Let the "direction" of a colorful patterned paper draw attention to your photo, like the arrow design on Carrie's page.

grass

playing in the

Summer is full of fun times especially when grandma is the playmate. Dinosaurs in the grass was even a fun game for Miss Claire. Tiny dinosaurs in the big wide open world of the backyard. summer 2005

Playing in the Grass by Carrie Owens. **Supplies** Textured cardstock and giant brads: Bazzill Basics Paper; Patterned paper: Scenic Route Paper Co.; Lettering: Carrie's own design.

tip On a two-page spread, use bolder patterns along the edges and simpler patterns in the center to help give the eye a resting place near the pictures in the middle.

tip Can't find the right accents to add a subtle look? Create your own! See how you can match the colors exactly to the ones in your photos with the directions below.

Wet and Wild Hooligans by Shannon Taylor. **Supplies** *Patterned papers:* BasicGrey; *Letter stickers:* American Crafts; *Metal-rimmed tag:* Tag Maker, Making Memories; *Transparencies:* Office Depot; *Adhesive:* Therm O Web; *Other:* Computer font.

To create patterned transparencies that match your photos perfectly:

1 Doodle a sun pattern with black marker on a clear transparency.

2 Scan your transparency, save it as a file and open it in a photo-editing program.

3 Open a photo in the photo-editing program and use the eyedropper tool to select a color from the photo.

4 Use your photo-editing program to fill the centers of the sun shapes with the selected color. Repeat using a second color as desired.

5 Print your updated paper on a transparency. ♥

coloring

OUTSIDE THE LINES

access your inner artist

Remember getting a new box of crayons each year as a child? This is one of my favorite back-to-school memories. I still love opening a new box of crayons and experiencing their rich colors, perfectly shaped tips and waxy smell. They hold the promise of purely creative play.

So, when's the last time you sat down with a box of crayons and let your creativity wander? How about watercolors or colored pencils? Now's the time to put aside that to-do list and play!

Come along as four scrapbook artists—Helen McCain, Pam Kopka, Tim Holtz and Britney Mellen—share four techniques they use to bring color and beauty to their pages. Follow their tips and remember—since you'll be creating your own lines, you won't need to stay in them!

by Heather Jones

GIGGLE *Tag by Tim Holtz.*
Supplies *Textured cardstock:* Bazzill Basics Paper; *Stamps:* Hero Arts and Catslife Press; *Stamping ink:* Ranger Industries; *Clip:* Design Originals; *Fabric and D-ring:* Junkitz; *Other:* Spray bottle, heat tool and acrylic paint.

HOME *Tag by Helen McCain.*
Supplies *Patterned paper:* Scenic Route Paper Co.; *Wood letters:* EK Success; *Stamping ink:* Ranger Industries; *Key charm:* Darice; *Vellum:* The Paper Company; *Colored pencils:* Crayola; *Other:* Corrugated cardstock, silk flowers and brads.

FLIGHT OF THE DRAGONFLY *Tag by Tim Holtz.*
Supplies *Textured cardstock:* Bazzill Basics Paper; *Stamping ink:* Ranger Industries; *Fabric, frame and acrylic accent:* Junkitz; *Rub-ons:* Chatterbox; *Other:* Eyelets, twig, stamps, mica, spray bottle and heat tool.

colored pencil perfection

Colored pencils create beautiful shading without becoming overbearing or exaggerated. You can use several colors to create custom colors or to induce darker and lighter tones as desired. This medium is perfect for a simple yet colorful look.

Helen McCain used traditional colored pencils and watercolor pencils here. By shading simple cotton fabric flowers, she created a whimsical and charming effect. Helen created the title with colored pencils by stamping the letters with paint, then tinting the dry paint with splashes of color.

SISTERS *by Helen McCain.*

Supplies *Patterned paper and sticker:* Scenic Route; *Colored pencils:* Prismacolor, Sanford; *Watercolor pencils:* Derwent; *Rubber stamps:* Leave Memories; *Acrylic paint, brads and photo turns:* Making Memories; *Transparency:* Grafix; *Ribbon:* May Arts; *Fiber:* BasicGrey; *Other:* Fabric.

To create the flowers:

1 Freeform your flower with a sewing machine. Begin by sewing an arc, then create a second arc, intersecting the first arc in the center. Continue until the flower is complete.

2 Cut out the flower and wet it. Remove the flower from the water, wad the flower up, unwad it and iron it. This will create a slightly fringed look around the edges and dry the material.

3 Color the flower with regular colored pencils or watercolor pencils. If using traditional colored pencils, simply color the fabric petals and shade with different colors as desired.

If using watercolor pencils (they'll create a darker base and paler petal tips), color them, then use a wet brush to spread the color to the rest of the fabric. Iron dry.

To create the title:

1 Using rubber stamps and acrylic paint, stamp a title onto a transparency or directly on paper.

2 When the paint has dried completely, start coloring along the edges of the letters to create nice definition. Partially color in the rest of each letter to complete the look.

watercolor whimsy

While traditional watercolor techniques involve tube or cake paints and can be tedious and time-consuming, you can pull off a similar look with today's "shortcut" products. For example, consider watercolor crayons. They're easy to use—simply color the area, wet it with a brush and you're done. The results? Stunning!

Pam Kopka's creativity here was sparked when teaching her kindergarten class. She noticed the students using watercolor crayons and loved the look. They quickly became a perfect medium for achieving a dreamy look without all the fuss and mess.

kara turns nine *by Pam Kopka.*
Supplies *Watercolor paper:* Canson; *Transparency:* Artistic Expressions; *Watercolor crayons:* Faber-Castell; *Marker:* American Crafts; *Rubber stamps:* Stampotique; *Stamping ink:* StazOn, Tsukineko; *Colored pencils:* Prismacolor, Sanford; *Fixative:* Krylon; *Adhesive spray:* 3M; *Clip art:* Softkey.

adore *by Pam Kopka.*
Supplies *Watercolor paper:* Canson; *Watercolor pencils:* Faber-Castell; *Stamping ink:* StazOn, Tsukineko; *Paint:* DecoArt; *Pens:* American Crafts; *Metal molds:* Ten Seconds Studio; *Gel medium:* Liquitex; *Stamps:* Wendi Speciale Designs; *Rub-ons:* Making Memories; *Adhesive:* Beacon Adhesive; *Other:* Fiber.

To create the background:

 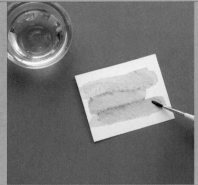

❶ Color area with watercolor crayons as desired.

❷ Wet a paintbrush and wash the colored area.

To create the flower:

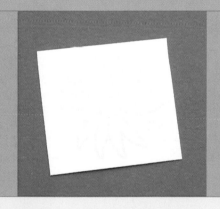  

❶ Select a clip-art image and change it to grayscale, printing the image on watercolor paper on the lightest setting.

❷ Color the image as desired with watercolor crayons.

❸ Using a damp paintbrush, trace over the crayon markings.

❹ Change the clip-art image to the black-and-white setting. Change print mode to "transparency" and print the image on a transparency.

❺ Spray the watercolor image with adhesive spray and attach the printed transparency, aligning the image outlines. Ink the edges as desired.

incredible inks

Color is so important to any paper-crafting project, and using ink is a great way to add design, shading and background effects. Working with water-based dye inkpads is a perfect start and, besides, they're easy to clean up!

Whether you're a seasoned stamper like Tim Holtz or a first-time ink user, this technique will have you designing like a pro with the look of hand-painted watercolor. An added bonus? You don't even need to pick up a paintbrush!

Picture *by Tim Holtz.*

Supplies *Textured cardstock:* Bazzill Basics Paper; *Textured woven paper:* Magic Scraps; *Stamping and distress inks:* Ranger Industries; *D-ring, brads and fabric:* Junkitz; *Bookplate:* Li'l Davis Designs.

To create the inked pattern:

  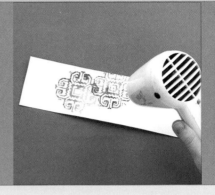

❶ If possible, remove an inkpad's lid by twisting it in the opposite direction from the body. (Some inkpads have removable lids that can be replaced.)

Using the corner of the inkpad, apply the ink to the desired area of the stamp image. Work from light to dark colors to avoid "dirtying" your inkpads. Repeat with additional colors until the image is completely colored with ink. Take your time with this step—it's OK if the ink dries on the stamp.

❷ Lay the stamp flat in your hand or on a flat surface, then mist the image directly with 3–4 sprays of water. The stamp should be very wet for this technique, so be generous with the water.

❸ Press the stamp down directly on textured paper and lift quickly. Immediately dry the wet image with a low-powered heat tool. (The Heat it Craft Tool by Ranger Industries is a good choice. More powerful heat guns can "blow" your ink around.) This step will dry the puddles of dye and water on the paper surface, creating a watercolor look.

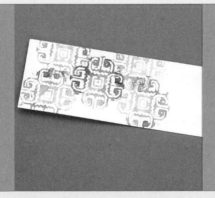 

❹ Repeat Steps 2 and 3 using the same inked stamp. The colors will last up to five additional stampings, getting lighter in color with each use.

Note: Stamp an entire sheet of paper for a wonderful background page.

❺ Embellish by tearing and inking the edges of the paper, then add it to your scrapbook page.

Punchy Paint

Just as a fresh coat of paint can brighten a room, a vibrant swipe of paint on a layout can make a bold statement. You don't always need to use bright colors to get your point across. Britney experimented with black and white to establish a contemporary, artistic feel.

Paint is extremely versatile, as shown in this layout by Britney. She masked her letters, then sponged and swiped over them, eventually revealing black lettering. Britney also drew a grid in the right-hand bottom corner and painted black squares to create the checkerboard pattern. ♥

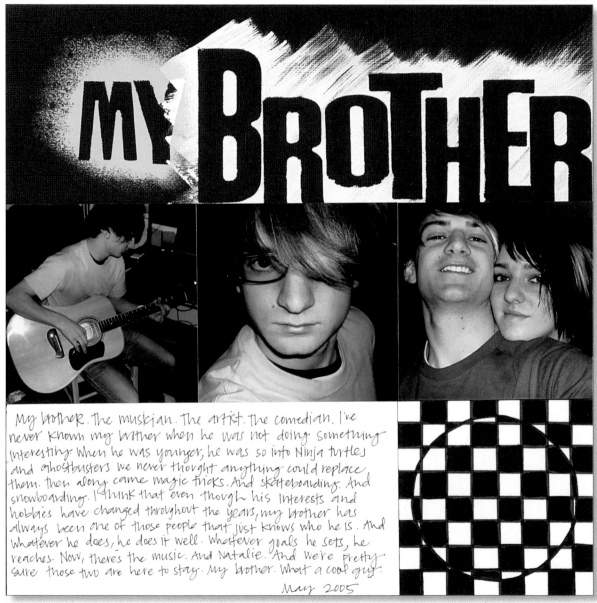

My brother. The musician. The artist. The comedian. I've never known my brother when he was not doing something interesting. When he was younger, he was so into Ninja turtles and Ghostbusters we never thought anything could replace them. then along came magic tricks. And skateboarding. And snowboarding. I think that even though his interests and hobbies have changed throughout the years, my brother has always been one of those people that just knows who he is. And whatever he does, he does it well. Whatever goals he sets, he reaches. Now, there's the music. And Natalie. And we're pretty sure those two are here to stay. My brother. What a cool guy.

May 2005

My Brother *by Britney Mellen.*
Supplies *Textured cardstock:* Bazzill Basics Paper; *Stickers:* Gin-X, Imagination Project; *Acrylic paint:* Making Memories; *Pen:* Pigma Micron, Sakura.

ROCK the CHALK

5 new ways to play

The instant I open a container of sidewalk chalk, my kids dive in. No hesitation. No worries about their design process, the possible outcome or the amount of time spent. They're ready to have fun.

The following contributors had fun as well experimenting with different ways to put chalk to cardstock. Whether developing new techniques or adding a twist to old ones, each discovered that part of loving your creation is loving its creation.

If you think chalk has lost its luster or feel frustrated by the pressure to create, now's a good time to relax and return to the childlike, worry-free days where you simply played. Chances are you already own some chalk, so let's dive in!

by Denise Pauley

airbrushing

Did you know you can use chalk and cutouts to create text, images and backgrounds with an airbrushed or spray-painted feel? As Pam Kopka shows here, it's easy!

Dreams *by Pam Kopka.* **Supplies** *Chalk:* EK Success; *Pen:* American Crafts; *Fixative:* Krylon; *Clip:* Nunn Design; *Computer font:* Brush, downloaded from the Internet; *Lettering:* Pam's own design.

To get this look:

❶ Coat a hand-cut letter with a good amount of chalk. *Hint:* This will also work with die cuts, punch-outs, punch pieces and more.

❷ Turn the letter over. Rub the color off onto your page, pushing outward and leaving a "negative image."

❸ Repeat with different shades of the same color for additional depth.

Variation:

To create a bright background, repeat the process several times across the cardstock with different colors of chalk, blending slightly where the shades meet.

Lettering can also be created by brushing or stippling chalk over templates or stencils. Create designs by placing painter's tape over a portion of the cardstock and applying chalk. Remove the tape and color the remainder, blending to soften the edges.

Be True *by Pam Kopka.* **Supplies** *Stickers:* The C-Thru Ruler Co.; *Embossing powder:* Ultra Thick Embossing Enamel, Ranger Industries; *Computer fonts:* Garamond, Microsoft Word; Love Letters, Enview and Myriad Web, downloaded from the Internet; *Other:* Fibers.

Cherish *by Pam Kopka.* **Supplies** *Flower:* Making Memories; *Sticker:* NRN Designs; *Brad:* Magic Scraps; *Chalk:* EK Success; *Other:* Ribbon.

faux paint

Want to create custom backgrounds and get the look of acrylic paint without the mess? You can! By simply removing and applying chalk with clear ink, plain cardstock can look like it's been painted, stamped and texturized.

She by Denise Pauley. **Supplies** *Cardstock:* DieCuts with A View; *Alphabet stamps and rub-ons:* Making Memories; *Rubber stamps:* Making Memories (large daisy) and Impress Rubber Stamps (smaller daisy); *Stamping ink:* ColorBox, Clearsnap; *Tab:* Autumn Leaves; *Chalk:* Deluxe Designs and The Stencil Company; *Pen:* American Crafts.

To get this look:

❶ Begin with a medium to dark shade of cardstock. Use textured cardstock for additional dimension.

❷ Cover the surface liberally with a light color of chalk. *Hint:* Chalky pastel sticks are ideal, but you can also remove a square of chalk from the palette and brush it against the cardstock. Note that this will use up a fair amount of chalk.

❸ Ink a rubber stamp with clear ink (I like VersaMark by Tsukineko). Press the stamp into the chalk to "lift" it away so the cardstock's original color can show through.

❹ To create the title, follow Step 3 with foam letter stamps. Take an applicator and brush over the images

lightly with chalk. This will make the letters pop with subtle dimension.

❺ To help set the chalk and "soften" the design for a more mottled, paint-like appearance, spray the chalk lightly with fixative. *Caution:* Too much spray may make the entire design disappear!

Variation:

For added interest and an even more abstract pattern, follow the steps for "chalk lifting," outlined above. While the ink is still wet, brush chalk lightly over a few of the flowers to create a background that has both light and dark images.

colorful backgrounds

Don't let the fact that you scrap on computer stop you from playing with chalk! Do what Cynthia Coulon does—create a colorful background on paper, then enhance the look in Photoshop before applying it to your layout.

Twelve by Cynthia Coulon. **Supplies** Computer software: Adobe Photoshop, Adobe Systems; Chalk: Pebbles Inc.; Stamping ink: Top Boss, Clearsnap; Letter stamps: Leave Memories; Computer fonts: Depraved and 4990810, downloaded from the Internet.

To get this look:

❶ Stamp the alphabet (or any other design) onto cardstock with clear embossing ink.

❷ Apply and blend different colors of chalk onto the stamped letters.

❸ Use this sheet as background paper. To create a digital version, scan the chalked design. Next, use photo-editing software to manipulate the hue and saturation levels to produce several different color combinations. Layer the pieces next to each other and on top of one another to create one "sheet" in the desired size.

Variation:

Achieve a similar look by tracing and coloring lettering templates or stencils with an embossing pen before chalking. You can also use computer fonts by outputting letters in light gray, then tracing them with the pen and brushing with chalk.

textured backgrounds

Follow Darcee Waddoups' lead and design textured backgrounds with touchable depth and custom colors. You can use any rough surface to create a pattern—simply use a bit of chalk to tint it. This technique is easy, eye-catching and economical!

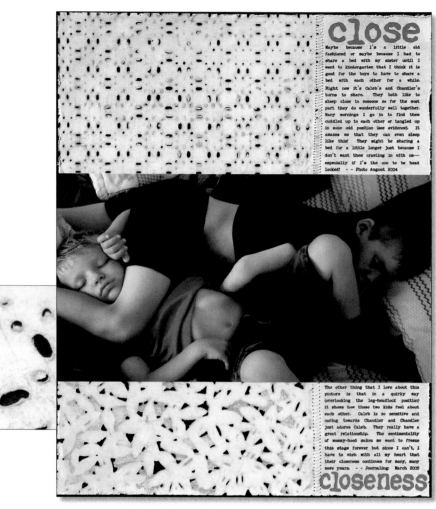

Closeness *by Darcee Waddoups.* **Supplies** *Chalk:* Deluxe Designs; *Texture templates:* Carolee's Creations and Scratch Art; *Computer font:* My Old Remington, downloaded from the Internet; *Other:* Thread.

To get this look:

❶ Affix a sheet of printer paper (any text-weight paper will work) to a texture template with low-tack tape.

❷ Run a chalk square over the paper, picking up the plate's texture.

❸ With the paper still taped to the template, lightly rub the surface with sandpaper for a slightly worn look. *Hint:* Be sure your sandpaper is clean; any color on it will transfer to your project.

❹ Rub chalk over the surface again to highlight the raised and torn areas.

Variation:

If you just want color to appear on the ridges, wait to apply chalk until after the paper has been texturized and sanded.

tinted photos

You don't need to invest in special materials to give photos a hand-tinted appearance. With a touch of chalk and the proper photo finish, you'll be achieving professional results in no time. Try one of these variations by Vicki Harvey.

Samples *by Vicki Harvey.* **Supplies** *Cardstock:* Bazzill Basics Paper; *Chalk:* Stampin' Up!; *Photo primer:* Marshall's.

For soft color, print your photo on flat matte paper, which has no sheen. *Hint:* If you can't find matte paper, try one of the other variations.

Apply chalk to the highlights with craft pom-poms attached to an "alligator" clip. Build up color as you go, rather than applying too much chalk at once.

For the look of tinted canvas, simply print a black-and-white photo on textured cardstock, then brush the areas you want to highlight lightly with chalk.

If your developer doesn't offer matte photos and you can't locate matte paper, pre-treat a glossy photo by spraying it with Marshall's Pre-Color Spray. The product will give the image a transparent matte finish. Tint the photo with chalk as desired, then apply another coat of spray to set the chalk. ❤

10 Sweet Chalk Tips

BY BRITNEY MELLEN

Dip into your chalk supply today!

One glimpse of a candy-colored chalk palette and I'm ready for a creative binge. Sound like fun? Read on—the following tips are the perfect indulgence for sweetening up your scrapbook pages. Treat yourself to one (or all) of these yummy techniques!

Customize letter stickers.

Chalk stencils are an easy way to add colors and patterns to plain stickers.

3

Family of ...

These are Creed's birth announcements. We had them letter-pressed by my friend Nicole. My friend Cathy took the photo. And yes those are Creed's little hands on the stamps!

creed

Family of 3 *by Britney Mellen. Photograph by Catherine Fegan-Kim.* **Supplies** *Cardstock:* Bazzill Basics Paper; *Number sticker:* Making Memories; *Chalk and stencil:* Pebbles Inc.; *Envelope:* Paper Source; *Pen:* Pigma Micron, Sakura; *Announcement:* Nicole LaRue.

Mama's Love *by C.D. Muckosky.* **Supplies** *Software:* Adobe Photoshop CS2, Adobe Systems; *Digital metal mesh and duct tape:* Katie Pertiet, *www.designerdigitals.com;* *Digital flower brads:* Jackie Eckles, *www.designerdigitals.com;* *Digital rickrack:* Kellie Mize, *www.designerdigitals.com; Round brads:* Kim Christensen, *www.scrapartist.com; Rickrack corner:* Tiff Brady, *www.plaindigitalwrapper.com; Address book tabs:* Misty Mareda, *www.plaindigitalwrapper.com; Other:* Silk flowers, chalk, ribbon and envelope.

Alter silk flowers.

Custom-colored silk flowers are only a few chalk swipes away. Try scanning altered flowers to create digital elements you can use again and again.

Think Big Thoughts by Amanda Probst. **Supplies** Cardstock: Bazzill Basics Paper; Chipboard frame: Scenic Route; Quote tag: My Mind's Eye; Rub-ons: Making Memories; Ink: Ranger Industries; Chalk: Craf-T Products; Font: Century Gothic, Microsoft Word.

Colorize rub-ons.

A light layer of chalk gives white rub-ons soft, subtle color.

Create custom patterned paper.

Lightly brush wet embossing ink with chalk to make stamped designs pop off the page.

Out of all
of your toys
lego is hands
down your favourite
It is not unusual
to find you lost
in legoland

lost in LEGO land

Lost in Legoland *by Vicki Boutin.* **Supplies** *Cardstock:* Bazzill Basics Paper; *Patterned papers:* Scenic Route; *Stamps:* gel-à-tins; *Chipboard letters:* Li'l Davis Designs; *Chalk:* Pebbles Inc.; *Ink:* VersaMark, Tsukineko; *Metal-rimmed tag:* Avery; *Marker:* Sharpie, Sanford; *Other:* Buttons.

Enhance stamped images.

Chalk pencils are the perfect solution for outlining or shading stamped images.

Jump by Robyn Werlich. **Supplies** *Patterned paper:* KI Memories; *Letter and flower stamps:* Autumn Leaves; *Dot stamp:* Stampotique Originals; *Chalk pencils:* General Pencil Co.; *Shimmer pastel chalks:* Pebbles Inc.; *Brads:* Autumn Leaves and Making Memories; *Ink:* Stampin' Up!; *Other:* Staples and thread.

Give computer-printed designs a boost.

Rub black-and-white printed designs with chalk for a dreamy wash of color. Spray a coat of fixative to prevent smearing.

Family by *Pam Kopka.* **Supplies** *Patterned papers:* Junkitz and Laguna; *Chipboard stickers and letter:* Die Cuts With a View; *Chipboard shapes:* Junkitz; *Chalk:* Pebbles Inc.; *Digital brushes:* Rhonna Farrer, *www.twopeasinabucket.com.*

Achieve a water-color look.

Mix water with ground-up chalk for instant "paint."

Flower by C.D. Muckosky. **Supplies** *Fabric flower:* Making Memories; *Pen:* Sharpie, Sanford; *Other:* Sidewalk chalk, water, hot glue, beads, safety pin, mesh, rickrack, paper clip and white paper.

Fashion an accent with suede-like texture.

Add chalk to chipboard with a sponge dauber for a velvety-soft finish.

Success Tag by Alicia Thelin for Stampin' Up!. **Supplies** *Stamps, cardstock, chipboard accents, ribbon, eyelet, button and chalk pastels:* Stampin' Up!; *Other:* Thread.

Create a rainbow of color.

Blending colors is a cinch with chalk pencils. Add a coat of dimensional glaze to lend a glossy shell to these candy-like accents and letters.

Smile by Robyn Werlich. **Supplies** *Patterned papers:* KI Memories, Creative Imaginations and Lasting Impressions for Paper; *Chalk pencils:* General Pencil Co.; *Die-cut letters:* QuicKutz; *Buttons:* Autumn Leaves; *Other:* Thread and dimensional glaze.

Modify die-cut shapes.

Don't have the right color of cardstock? Colorize white die cuts and punched shapes with chalk! ♥

Thank You Very Much by Amy Yingling for Stampin' Up!. **Supplies** *Stamps, cardstock, ink, chalk pastels, twill tape, thread, photo turn and brads:* Stampin' Up!; *Other:* Thread.

WATERCOLOR STAMPING

GET A "WOW" LOOK IN 4 SIMPLE STEPS

ALL MY LIFE I've dreamed of being an artist. I've pictured myself creating lovely watercolors that people will admire for years to come. The problem? Every time I've picked up a brush and tried my hand at watercolor, the results haven't matched the vision.

You can imagine my delight the day I discovered an easy way to create watercolor masterpieces with rubber stamps.

by Jennifer McGuire

WHILE the results look difficult to achieve, the process is actually quite simple! (Don't you love shortcuts like this?) In just four steps, you can create watercolor looks that are perfect for your precious family photos. Let's get started! . . . .

Every single day of your life, you read. Not only do you read, you get completely absorbed in your books. Captivated. Immersed. Engaged. It is amazing.

eVeRy siNgle DaY

Add a dramatic touch by combining light and dark watercolor looks. *Page by Jennifer McGuire.* **Supplies** *Textured cardstock:* Bazzill Basics Paper; *Rubber stamps and watercolors:* Hero Arts; *Computer font:* Arial, Microsoft Word; *Other:* Thread.

WATERCOLOR STAMPING

The watercolor stamping process is similar to regular stamping, except the ink is painted on instead of applied with a stamp pad. Here's how to do it:

1 Freshen up a new or used rubber stamp by wiping it with a damp baby wipe or ink cleaner. This will help when applying the watercolor.

2 Apply watercolor to a thin paintbrush, then paint any stamp sections desired with watercolor. *Note:* If your stamp has multiple sections, repeat this step for each portion with a different color until complete (see the flower images on page 184).

3 Spritz the painted rubber stamp lightly with a water mister, holding the mister about one foot from the stamp.

4 Stamp the image onto the project. If the image fails to stamp completely, fill in open areas with a paintbrush and watercolor.

Watercolor stamping is that easy! And remember, practice makes perfect—so attempt the process a few times before using the technique on your actual layouts.

WATERCOLOR TIPS

The more you experiment with this technique, the more you'll pick up tips to help achieve your desired look. Here are a few of my favorites:

• **Combine light and dark images for a dramatic touch.** To create the background images in the strips on "Every Single Day" (see page 182), I applied more water to my paints before adding them to my rubber stamps. To create the bolder designs in the strips' foreground, I used less water with my paints.

• **Keep several paintbrushes on hand so each can be dedicated to a single color.** I tie a colored ribbon to the end of each handle (see brushes at left) to represent the color of paint it's used for. This simple trick helps me avoid accidentally putting a brush into the wrong watercolor and creating a mess.

Stamp several "watercolor" images onto cardstock, then cut them into strips for an eye-catching border. *Page by Jennifer McGuire.*
Supplies *Patterned papers and dimensional letter sticker:* K&Company; *Photo corner punch:* EK Success; *Stamps and watercolors:* Hero Arts; *Brads:* Making Memories; *Pen:* American Crafts; *Computer font:* Chauncy, downloaded from the Internet.

Idea to note: To call attention to her daughter's smile and eyes, Jennifer copied a portion of the main photo and cropped it into a block. She then added it to her watercolor border for a finishing touch.

Great border look!

TRY IT YOURSELF!

What else can you do with this technique? See what Ali Edwards, Renee Camacho and Marilyn Healey came up with, each adding their own special touches! • • • •

create a **GRAPHIC LOOK**

Good morning sweet Simon boy.

Cool combination of artistic and graphic!

Unite graphic stamps and artistic techniques for a sensational design. *Page by Ali Edwards.* **Supplies** *Textured cardstock:* Bazzill Basics Paper; *"S" letter:* Autumn Leaves; *Rubber stamps:* FontWerks: *Watercolor paints:* Loew-Cornell; *Pen:* American Crafts.

"Don't worry about exactness with watercolor stamping. The slight mess is part of the charm."
—Ali Edwards

ALI'S NOTES

It's fun when you can dip into your child's art supplies for a creative twist. Plus, I love the imperfections of the watercolor paint on the stamps. In creating a background pattern for this page, I loved how the stamp design looked like each dot was placed down on its own. Each circle is imperfect and beautiful in its own right.

COMBINE TECHNIQUES for a cool twist

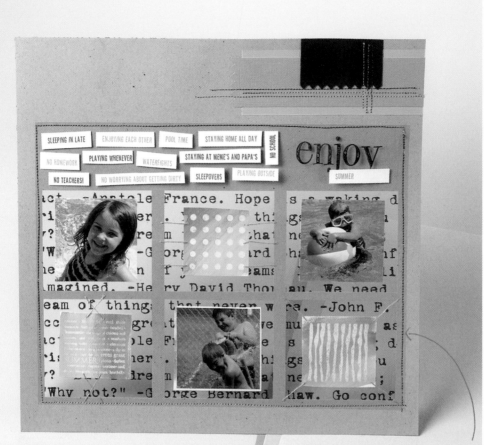

Idea to note:
Renee adhered her layout over a text-printed transparency.

Fun window idea!

Combine watercolor stamping with other favorite techniques, like resist. **Page by Renee Camacho. Supplies** *Textured cardstock:* Making Memories; *Watercolor paper:* Canson; *Transparencies:* K&Company and Office Depot; *Decorative scissors:* EK Success; *Rubber stamps and watercolors:* Hero Arts; *Stamping ink:* StazOn, Tsukineko; Ranger Industries; *Embossing powder:* Paper Moon; *Computer font:* 2Peas Tasklist, downloaded from www.two-peasinabucket.com; *Other:* Thread.

RENEE'S NOTES

I knew that watercolor paints over a resisted image would provide a subtle yet dynamic burst of color. To create this page, I resisted, then painted over an entire piece of watercolor paper before trimming it into blocks of various sizes. The look of "painting" over a resisted image provides a large block of watercolor with the stamped image on the inside.

"I love the look of watercolor painting. It has a softer appearance than inks do when used with stamping. The technique makes your artwork appear exactly like that—art."
—Renee Camacho

JAZZ **UP** your journaling

Add a hand-painted look to your journaling blocks with watercolor stamping.
Pages by Marilyn Healey. **Supplies** *Rubber stamps:* Ma Vinci's Reliquary (letters), Stampers Anonymous, Dewey, Inkum & Howe, Hero Arts and Hampton Art; *Pen:* Zig Writer, EK Success.

> "I like the missing-in-places, washy look of the technique."
> —Marilyn Healey

MARILYN'S TECHNIQUE

Marilyn adapted the technique by using it as a background for her journaling. The colorful design draws readers' eyes to the text without overwhelming the writing. ♥

totally tempting tip

Add Punch with Paint

Draw shapes on patterned papers with fabric paint, then cut them out once they're dry to create fun embellishments! The thick fabric paint makes the accents three-dimensional. I use it to add punch to a page.
—*Elsie Flannigan, Springfield, MO* ❤

Bliss *by Elsie Flannigan.* **Supplies** *Patterned papers:* BasicGrey; *Rub-ons:* Li'l Davis Designs; *Pen:* Uni-ball Signo, Sanford; *Other:* Fabric paint.

FUN

WITH
Foam Brushes

Alter them for fantastic effects

BY HEIDI STEPANOVA

I love a good bargain! When I find a craft supply that's both inexpensive *and* versatile, I'm ecstatic. I was thrilled with acrylic paints—then things got even better when I noticed a bin of foam brushes on the aisle. The price was low and the brushes were disposable (I love any supply I can throw away instead of clean up), so I picked up a dozen. Little did I know how handy these little brushes would be. Before I knew it, I was altering the basic foam brushes to create all kinds of stamped, striped, streaked and sponged looks. Grab a brush and try these fun, fresh techniques. ➜

TECHNIQUE 1: Simple Shapes

You can apply paint with the tip of your brush, but don't stop there. Instead, look at your brush from a different perspective to create dozens of shaped effects.

Turn the brush on its side, and you'll see a natural tag shape that's perfect for stamping. Cut off the slanted tip, and the brush becomes a square suited for painting a checkerboard. You can also remove the tip and cut other shapes to create custom stamps. Just be careful to plan your shape around the handle and the plastic insert that hold the brush together.

Paint multiple tag looks by using various brush sizes.

Supplies *Textured cardstock:* Bazzill Basics Paper; *Acrylic paints and foam stamps:* Making Memories; *Alphabet stamps:* River City Rubber Works; *Gold-leafing pen:* Krylon; *Stamping ink:* StazOn, Tsukineko; *Computer fonts:* Bradley Hand ITC and Calisto MT, downloaded from the Internet.

Create a tag shape by turning a foam brush on its side.

Cut off the end of a foam brush to create a square stamp.

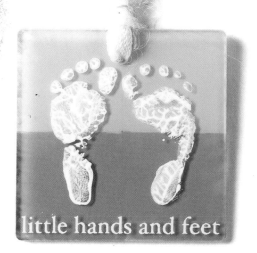

little hands and feet

Turn your foam brush into a square sponge to color–block the back of a clear tag.

Supplies *Tag:* Creek Bank Creations; *Acrylic paints and rub-ons:* Making Memories; *Fibers:* Adornments, EK Success; *Other:* Stamp.

Experiment with your brush to design other stamping shapes.

TECHNIQUE 2: Sensational Stripes

You can also alter your brushes to create multiple stripes with a single brush stroke. I made casual, uneven stripes and funky, striped circles below by wrapping one brush with rubber bands and placing brads in the tip of another. The rubber bands and brads make the foam pucker and prevent part of the brush from hitting the paper with light pressure.

If you want evenly spaced stripes like these below, consider cutting notches into your brush with regular or decorative scissors. Create varied looks by experimenting with the amount of pressure used.

Create fun striped effects by wrapping rubber bands around a foam brush and dragging it in wavy patterns across a layout.

Supplies *Textured cardstock:* Bazzill Basics Paper; *Acrylic paint and rub-ons:* Making Memories; *Letter stickers:* Pioneer Photo Albums; *Ribbon:* C.M. Offray & Son; *Photo turns:* Creek Bank Creations; *Charm and epoxy letter:* Li'l Davis Designs; *Other:* Brads.

Heidi painted the brads and the edges of the white photo mats to match the swirls she painted on the bottom block.

Rubber bands provide a quick solution for creating multiple stripes at once.

To create parallel stripes when you paint, pin back part of the brush tip with a small brad.

Last chance to rise and shine!

Typical bedtime

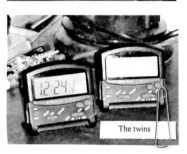

The twins

Why, you might ask, would anyone have four alarm clocks? Everyone has one, and many people even have two, but four seems a bit extreme, if not just downright anal. But my alarm clocks and I have a very special relationship, and I can't imagine life with just one of them.

The truth is that I'm not a hop-out-of-bed-and-go-running-to-face-the-day type of person. I'm a hit-the-snooze-bar-20-times type of person. I prefer to wake up slowly, to take a few minutes and appreciate the comfort of my soft, warm bed and to adjust to reality on my own terms and at my own pace. So where do the four alarm clocks enter into the picture? They help me transition into my day in small, easy installments. My little white alarm clock is the first to go off with a very high but soft beep. Unfortunately, this clock is highly unreliable and has a very short 2-minute snooze. Since 2 minutes of sleep is not enough time to really appreciate my bed, so I usually turn it right off at the first beep. The twins go off next, 5 minutes apart. They have a 7 minute snooze cycle, and usually after 2 or 3 beeps I'm ready to get up. My last alarm clock and I have a love-hate relationship. He's always set for the last possible minute that I can get out of bed and be where I need to be, and while I truly hate his increasing volume, hideously obnoxious beep, he never lets me down (he even has a battery back-up). I'm deeply grateful for all the mornings when I've slept through the little guys, and he's saved my day by forcing me, ungrateful and grumbling, out of bed.

So I have four alarm clocks. My husband, a go-running type of guy, will probably never understand how the incessant beeping that drives him nuts is a gentle transition for me. I, on the other hand, will never understand how he can hop out of bed on the first beep. I will, however, always be grateful to my little clocks for their patience, persistence, and dedicated service.

To create bold painted looks, add a brad (see the bottom border) to your brush or trim notches into your brush (see the top border).

Supplies *Acrylic paint:* Delta Creative; *Epoxy letters:* Li'l Davis Designs; *Letter stickers:* Pioneer Photo Albums and Making Memories; *Rub-ons:* Making Memories and Creative Imaginations; *Computer font:* Times New Roman, Microsoft Word; *Other:* Paper clips and black pen.

Heidi followed a wave template while painting the top border. To create the circles around the "beep" letters on the bottom border, she temporarily adhered circle punches to the paper as a mask, then painted the stripes with heavy pressure.

Use a notched brush to create simple wave patterns.

TECHNIQUE 3: Bold Patterns

You can even use your brushes to achieve other geometric patterns. If you cut your brush parallel to the long outside edges of the tip (about ¼" from each edge) and remove the wide inner flap, you'll create a brush that looks like a Batman silhouette (see below).

To obtain an evenly spaced row of stylized triangles with this brush, lightly load the "ear" flaps with paint, then stamp the brush perpendicular to your paper. The flaps will fold under to create triangles. To create circle designs, simply hold one flap still while rotating the other flap around it.

With both techniques, you may need to practice a bit before you achieve perfect shapes. Want one more great trick? If you'd rather have a decorative background than printed patterns, create a sponged look by ripping away tiny pieces of the brush tip.

Stamped triangles provide a decorative background for tags. To make a diamond print, Heidi painted two rows of triangles side by side.

Supplies *Textured cardstock:* Bazzill Basics Paper; *Acrylic paint:* Delta Technical Coatings; *Rub-ons:* Making Memories; *Glass beads:* Provo Craft; *Fiber:* Fibers By The Yard; *Other:* Lace, ribbon, flower and brad.

Create rows of small triangles with two flaps on the outside edges of your brush.

Tear away small pieces from the brush tip to create a sponged look when you paint.

Supplies *Acrylic paints and rub-ons:* Making Memories; *Computer font:* Times New Roman, Microsoft Word; *Other:* Brads.

Dip only one flap of your Batman brush in paint and rotate the brush around the inner flap to create circle patterns.

The next time you're in a craft store, pick up a few foam brushes with your pocket change. You can have fun trying the techniques shared here, or look for other ways to alter your brushes. If you're really up for a creative challenge, try the techniques here on a sponge roller! No matter what types of brushes and alterations you use, you're bound to come up with fun outcomes. You'll never look at foam brushes the same way again! ❤

tool time
pens & markers

heartfelt

Before you were conceived, I wanted you. Before you were born, I loved you. Before you were here an hour, I would die for you. This is the miracle of life.

~ Maureen Hawkins

FINE & CHISEL

jot this down! | by JENNIFER MCGUIRE

SAY "SUPPLIES," and you and I tend to think of the cardstock, paper and embellishments we use every day. But what about the tools at the heart of scrapbooking? I'm talking about pens, punches, stamps, stencils—you name it. Not only are they proven performers, they're packed with potential. You can use the tools for basic tasks, or take them to a totally new level by adding creative twists. >

Here, I've used a handful of tools every scrapbooker has: pens and markers. I must admit—previously I'd rarely used them for more than lettering since I'm not much of an illustrator. But I learned an important lesson: You don't need to be an illustrator to create fun results! Give these 12 ideas a try.

Doodle on paper-pieced accents to unify various paper colors and designs.

< **Dear Jana** by Jennifer McGuire. **Supplies** *Patterned papers:* K&Company; foof-a-La, Autumn Leaves; Doodlebug Design; *Printed transparency:* Creative Imaginations; *Buttons:* Doodlebug Design; *Letter stickers:* Chatterbox; *Black pen:* American Crafts; *Other:* Thread.

Doodle *within* lines and circles on patterned papers!

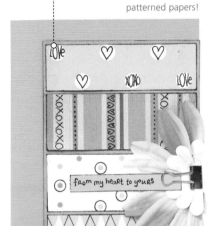

∧ **From My Heart to Yours** *Card* by Jennifer McGuire. **Supplies** *Note card:* Hero Arts; *Patterned papers:* Chatterbox, SEI and American Crafts; *Paper flower:* Making Memories; *Silk flower:* Hobby Lobby; *Rubber stamps:* Impress Rubber Stamps; *Stamping ink:* Memories, Stewart Superior Corporation; *Pens:* American Crafts; *Other:* Binder clip.

Trace products to create outlined designs.
Think die-cut letters, transparent shapes, masks and more!

∧ **Mom** by Jennifer McGuire. **Supplies** *Patterned papers:* Chatterbox, K&Company and Scrapworks; *Die-cut letters for tracing:* KI Memories; *Clear acetate hearts and floral mask for tracing:* Heidi Swapp for Advantus; *Gems:* Hero Arts; *Paper flowers:* Prima; *Pens:* Staedtler (brown) and Sharpie, Sanford (white); *Other:* Thread.

Pens courtesy of American Crafts, EK Success, Marvy Uchida, Staedtler and Tombow.

Moment
Scribble markers over white rub-ons, then quickly wipe with a paper towel for a unique resist.

Supplies *Rub-on:* Déjà Views by The C-Thru Ruler Co.; *Pin:* Junkitz; *Ribbon:* May Arts; *Markers:* Tombow; *Other:* Lace, tag and thread.

Before
Use pens to achieve rounded journaling that can be difficult with computer fonts.

Supplies *Patterned papers:* KI Memories and K&Company; *Rubber stamps and buttons:* Hero Arts; *Flower:* Doodlebug Design; *Pens:* American Crafts; *Other:* Thread.

Heartfelt
Outline shapes with marker, then quickly blend with a wet paintbrush to "paint" like watercolor.

Supplies *Cardstock:* Bazzill Basics Paper; *Rubber stamps:* Hero Arts; *Stamping ink:* Memories, Stewart Superior Corporation; *Markers:* Marvy Uchida; *Other:* Ribbon and thread.

Together
Transform cardstock by doodling with a darker-tone marker.*

Supplies *Cardstock:* Bazzill Basics Paper; *Buttons:* foof-a-La, Autumn Leaves; *Image accent ("together"):* American Crafts; *Markers:* Evanscraft; *Other:* Faux silk flowers and thread.

* Achieve a similar look with a watermark pen and heat embossing.

Bless
Use stickers as a mask.
Doodle over them, then remove.

Supplies *Cardstock:* Bazzill Basics Paper; *Letter stickers (for masking):* American Crafts; *Button:* Doodlebug Design; *Rubber stamps:* Hero Arts; *Stamping ink:* Memories, Stewart Superior Corporation; *Markers:* Zig Writer, EK Success; *Other:* Thread.

Darling
Draw patterns on ribbon,
flowers, chipboard accents and
more for a new look.

Supplies *Cardstock:* Bazzill Basics Paper; *Patterned paper and chipboard heart:* Gin-X, Imagination Project; *Paper flowers:* Prima; *Rub-ons:* Déjà Views by The C-Thru Ruler Co.; *Gems:* Hero Arts; *Pens and markers:* Sharpie, Sanford (white) and Marvy Uchida (colored); *Other:* Ribbon, photo corners and rickrack.

J
Help transparent letters "pop"
by coloring the edges with pen.

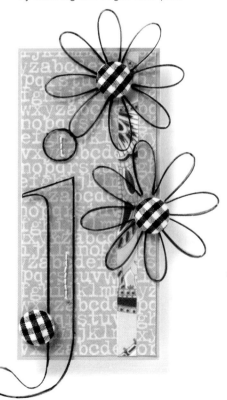

Supplies *Patterned papers:* KI Memories and NRN Designs; *Clear acetate shapes:* Heidi Swapp for Advantus; Autumn Leaves; *Fabric brads:* Accent Depot, Hot Off The Press; *Pen:* Slick Writer, American Crafts; *Other:* Thread.

Three Hearts
Draw faux stitching and sewing.
Poke holes to enhance the effect.

Supplies *Patterned papers:* Anna Griffin, Making Memories and Autumn Leaves; *Metal-rimmed tags and tag maker:* Making Memories; *Pens:* Zig Writer, EK Success (colored) and Sharpie, Sanford (white); *Other:* Ribbon, charm and staples.

tool time

seeing clearly

seeing clearly! | by JENNIFER MCGUIRE

For this Tool Time, I played with clear inks, including watermark, embossing and resist varieties. You can do so many things with them—love that!

They can be used alone, for embossing or with other products. It's time to have some fun. Pick your favorite idea and try it today!

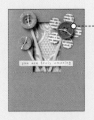

Meeting Bryn by Jennifer McGuire. **Supplies** *Clear stamping ink:* VersaMark, Tsukineko; *Textured cardstock:* Bazzill Basics Paper; *Rubber stamps:* Hero Arts and JudiKins; *Patterned papers:* Chatterbox; *Ribbon and epoxy "sweet" accent:* American Crafts; *Other:* Thread and rhinestone flowers.

Create background papers by watermark-stamping with clear ink. To create a diamond pattern, press a small watermark ink cube directly onto the paper—repeat to form lines. To add intensity, heat emboss with clear powder.

Change the color of embellishments by covering with clear ink, adding embossing powder and heating. (Be sure to use tweezers!)

Amazing by Jennifer McGuire. **Supplies** *Clear stamping ink:* VersaMark, Tsukineko; *Patterned papers:* Anna Griffin (pink) and unknown (vintage); *Rubber stamp:* Hero Arts; *Buttons:* Buttons Galore; *Embossing powder:* Tim Holtz Distress Powder, Ranger Industries; *Other:* Thread. *See larger version of card on page 200.*

Change the color and look of light patterned papers with watercolor resist. Just stamp on the patterned paper with clear ink, heat emboss, then paint over with watercolor and wipe away any excess.

Come Walk with Me by Jennifer McGuire. **Supplies** *Clear stamping ink:* Top Boss, Clearsnap; *Textured cardstock:* Bazzill Basics Paper; *Patterned papers:* foof-a-La, Autumn Leaves; Daisy D's Paper Co.; *Watercolor, embossing powder and rubber stamps:* Hero Arts; *Computer font:* AL Singsong, "15 Script Fonts" CD, Autumn Leaves; *Other:* Buttons and thread.

Try These Inks
Check out these clear ink options:

• Palette Embossing & Watermark, Stewart Superior Corporation
www.stewartsuperior.com

• Perfect Medium, Ranger Industries
www.rangerink.com

• Top Boss, Clearsnap
www.clearsnap.com

• VersaMark, Tsukineko
www.tsukineko.com

I Luv U
Spice up plain chipboard
pieces by stamping subtle
watermark images.

Supplies *Clear stamping ink:* VersaMark, Tsukineko;
Chipboard tags: Daisy D's Paper Co.; *Ribbons:* C.M.
Offray & Son and May Arts; *Metal letter:* Making
Memories; *Rubber Stamps:* Hero Arts and JudiKins;
Black stamping ink: Memories, Stewart Superior
Corporation.

Joy
Use acrylic paint for a unique resist look.
(Stamp first with resist ink, then paint and
wipe away excess.)

Supplies *Clear stamping ink:* VersaMark, Tsukineko; *Sequins:* Doodlebug
Design; *Acrylic paint:* Delta Creative; *Ribbon:* May Arts; *Metal-rimmed
tags:* Tag Maker, Making Memories; *Computer font:* 2Peas Secret Pal,
downloaded from www.twopeasinabucket.com; Century Gothic,
Microsoft Word; *Other:* Twine, patterned paper and brad.

Chase Life
Brush clear stamped images
with Pearl-Ex for an iridescent look.

Supplies *Clear stamping ink:* VersaMark, Tsukineko; *Textured card-
stock:* Bazzill Basics Paper; *Rubber stamps:* Wordsworth, JudiKins and
Stampington & Co., Somerset Studios; *Powder:* Pearl-Ex, Jacquard
Products; *Ribbon:* May Arts; *Brads:* Making Memories.

Shine
Rub a clear inkpad directly
over textured paper to enhance
the pattern.

Supplies *Clear stamping ink:* Palette Embossing &
Watermark, Stewart Superior Corporation; *Textured
cardstock:* Bazzill Basics Paper; *Patterned paper:* Anna
Griffin; *Sun embellishment:* K&Company; *Quote sticker:*
Cloud 9 Design; *Photo turn:* Hero Arts; *Other:* Thread.

Faith

Lay down a mask, then press clear ink over remaining area. Emboss for a textured background.

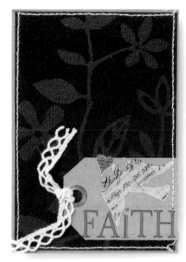

Supplies *Clear stamping ink:* Top Boss, Clearsnap; *Embossing powder:* Hero Arts; *Mask:* Heidi Swapp for Advantus; *Rub-ons:* K&Company; *Lace:* Making Memories; *Other:* Thread.

Memories

Stamp with clear ink and rub with chalk to add soft color.

Supplies *Clear stamping ink:* Palette Embossing & Watermark, Stewart Superior Corporation; *Textured cardstock:* Bazzill Basics Paper; *Rubber stamps:* Hero Arts; *Chalk:* Craf-T Products; *Flourish accents:* Autumn Leaves; *Ribbon:* May Arts; *Other:* Paper bag envelope, plastic tab and button.

Happiness

Create shadows for stamped color images by stamping with clear ink before rotating and using the colored inkpads.

Supplies *Clear stamping ink:* VersaMark, Tsukineko; *Textured cardstock:* Bazzill Basics Paper; *Rubber stamps:* Hero Arts and Rubbermoon Stamp Company; *Colored stamping ink:* Memories, Stewart Superior Corporation; *Other:* Buttons, ribbon and thread.

Europe

Protect embellishments on a mini-album cover by: 1) covering with clear ink and 2) heat embossing and repeating several times. Add photos after heat embossing if you don't want them embossed. ♥

Supplies *Clear stamping ink:* Top Boss, Clearsnap; *Mini album:* Tim Holtz Ruler Books, Junkitz; *Rub-ons:* Autumn Leaves; *Patterned paper:* Daisy D's Paper Co.; *Other:* Vintage postage, ribbon and jute.

tool time
rubber stamps

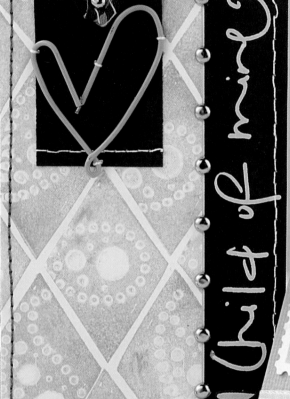

ready, set, stamp! | by JENNIFER MCGUIRE

Want to get more mileage from your rubber stamps? As someone who's stamped for years and has quite a collection (everything from basic shapes to greetings), I've had ample opportunity to experiment. Here are 12 ideas you're sure to enjoy!

Stamp soft images in white or clear ink on plain cardstock, then heat emboss for added punch.

Stamp images on a white background with clear pigment ink, then add generous colors of chalk one at a time with a soft make-up applicator or your fingertip.

Cut out stamped images and piece them into a design.

Welcome, Sweet Samuel. **Supplies** *Patterned papers:* Chatterbox and KI Memories; *Letter stickers:* American Crafts; *Rub-ons:* Making Memories; *Rubber stamps and clear embossing powder:* Hero Arts; *Stamping Ink:* Brilllance and VersaMark, Tsukineko; *Computer font:* AL Uncle Charles, "15 Essential Fonts" CD, Autumn Leaves; *Other:* Buttons and twine. XOXO. **Supplies** *Textured cardstock:* Bazzill Basics Paper; *Circle paper:* Autumn Leaves; *Large metal photo corner:* Scrapworks; *Metal charm and safety pin:* Making Memories; *Flowers:* Doodlebug Design; *Rubber stamps:* Hero Arts; *Stamping ink:* VersaMark, Tsukineko; *Chalk:* Craf-T Products; *Computer font:* Century Gothic, Microsoft Word; *Other:* Brads, ribbon, thread and rickrack.
Cherish. **Supplies** *Brads:* Making Memories; *Rubber stamps:* Hero Arts; *Stamping ink:* VersaMark, Tsukineko; *Other:* Thread..

Create cool resist images on the glossy side of a merchandise tag!

Supplies *Patterned paper:* Chatterbox; *Merchandise tag:* Office Depot; *Word label:* Jo-Ann Scrap Essentials; *Heart punches:* EK Success; *Ribbon:* C.M. Offray & Son; *Button:* Doodlebug Design; *Rubber stamps:* Hero Arts; *Stamping ink:* Ranger Industries (resist); ColorBox, Clearsnap; StazOn, Tsukineko; *Other:* Thread.

Add sparkle! Apply glue to a stamp's rubber, stamp on paper, then shake glitter over the wet glue.

Supplies *Textured cardstock:* Bazzill Basics Paper; *Chipboard bookplate:* Making Memories; *Word label:* me & my BIG ideas; *Heart button:* Doodlebug Design; *Photo turn:* Junkitz; *Brad:* American Tag; *Rubber stamp and glitter:* Hero Arts; *Liquid glue:* EK Success; *Other:* Patterned paper, ribbon and thread.

Stitch around an image (by hand or sewing machine) to set it off.

Supplies *Textured cardstock:* Bazzill Basics Paper; *Acrylic tag:* Junkitz; *Flower button:* Impress Rubber Stamps; *Ribbon:* Stampin' Up!; *Rubber stamps:* Hero Arts; *Stamping ink:* VersaMark (background) and VersaColor (flower), Tsukineko; *Other:* Thread.

Ink one stamp with pigment ink, then press a non-inked stamp on the rubber. Stamp with either on your project!

Supplies *Rub-ons:* Déjà Views by The C-Thru Ruler Co.; *Ribbon:* American Crafts; *Brads:* American Tag; *Rubber stamps:* Hero Arts; *Stamping ink:* VersaMark, Tsukineko; *Other:* Pink paper clip and thread.

Keep it soft with chalk resist on an embossed image.

Supplies *Textured cardstock:* Bazzill Basics Paper; *Chalk pencils:* Creatacolor; *Brads:* Making Memories; *Letter beads:* Hobby Lobby; *Safety pins:* Creative Impressions; *Rubber stamps and embossing powder:* Hero Arts; *Stamping ink:* Brilliance, Tsukineko; *Other:* Ribbon.

Stamp on fabric with white pigment ink and heat emboss with white powder.

Supplies *Printed ribbon:* Making Memories; *Rubber stamps and embossing powder:* Hero Arts; *Stamping ink:* Brilliance, Tsukineko; *Other:* Fabric, beads, hatpins and pink ribbon.

Personalize a transparency by stamping on it repeatedly with solvent ink.

Supplies *Transparency:* Office Depot; *Textured paper:* FiberMark; *Rubber stamps:* Rubbermoon Stamp Company and Hero Arts; *Stamping ink:* StazOn, Tsukineko; *Other:* Twine and crocheted flower.

Create faux postage that's fab! ♥

Supplies *Textured cardstock:* Bazzill Basics Paper; *Decorative scissors:* Postage edge, Fiskars; *Buttons:* Doodlebug Design; *Rubber stamps:* Hero Arts; *Stamping ink:* VersaColor, Tsukineko; *Other:* Ribbon and thread.

tool time
masking tools

Make It Cool with Masks | by JENNIFER MCGUIRE

I love masks! Not the costume kind, but those that let you create cool looks with some "white space." You'll find masking tools everywhere—from specifically marked products to items in your stash that you might not have considered (I'll show you!). To be honest, I have several masks and masking products but hadn't played with them much. Once I started using them, I quickly became addicted. Here are 12 ideas to inspire you!

Place alphabet masks on patterned paper and dab colored ink on top with a make-up applicator. Don't have alphabet masks? Use letter stickers instead (place them lightly), removing once inked.

Samuel *by Jennifer McGuire.* **Supplies** *Letter masks:* Heidi Swapp; *Stamping ink:* Tim Holtz Distress Ink, Ranger Industries; *Patterned papers:* Chatterbox ("a"), KI Memories ("m" and "l"), Doodlebug Design ("u") and Paperfever ("e"); *Metal-rimmed tags:* Tag Maker, Making Memories; *Other:* Binder clip, ribbon and vintage book paper ("s").

I'll Never Leaf You *by Jennifer McGuire.* **Supplies** *Stamps:* Hero Arts; *Other:* Charm, brad and thread.

Use sticky notes as masks to stamp images close together without messy overlapping! Stamp an image once onto the card and once onto a sticky note. Cut out the image from the sticky note. Stamp the sticky-note image over the card image and stamp the next image over it. Repeat for each stamped image.

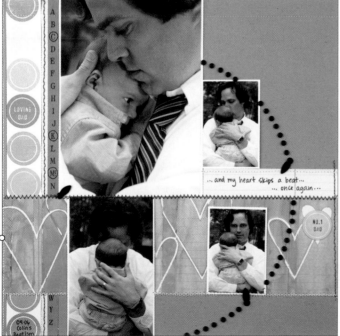

Once Again *by Jennifer McGuire.* **Supplies** *Heart stencil masks:* Heidi Swapp for Advantus; *Patterned papers and rub-ons:* Autumn Leaves; *Acrylic paint:* Delta Creative; *Other:* Brad, stamping ink, thread, photo turns and sticky notes.

Create your own striped and patterned papers! Apply heart-stencil masks to paper. Use sticky notes to create vertical lines and paint in one color; let dry. Remove sticky notes, reposition (or use new ones) and repeat with different colors as desired. Once complete, remove heart-stencil masks.

Almost any product can serve as a masking tool. Keep these items (from top left to bottom right) in mind for your next project:

- Premade masks/stencils (consider Heidi Swapp for Advantus)
- Masking fluid (such as bottles from Dr. Ph. Martin's or pens from Masqupen)
- Assorted tools and embellishments (like punches, frames and stickers)
- Masking tape

ONLINE BONUS
Learn to mask with our free how-to videos! Visit *www.creatingkeepsakes.com/alphamasks* and *www.creatingkeepsakes.com/stampmasks* today.

Colin and Roxie
Use the leftover negatives of
letter stickers as masks.

Supplies *Letter sticker negatives:* Doodlebug Design;
Stamps: Hero Arts; *Metal-rimmed tag and metal charm:*
Making Memories; *File folder:* Autumn Leaves; *Stamping
ink:* VersaColor, Tsukineko; *Ribbon:* KI Memories; *Other:*
Staples and thread.

Little A
Lay a stencil mask down,
then stamp over it.

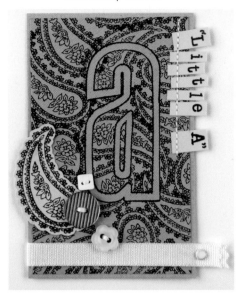

Supplies *Letter stencil mask:* Heidi Swapp for
Advantus; *Stamps:* Just Rite (letter) and Hero Arts
(paisley); *Buttons:* Autumn Leaves; *Other:* Ribbon,
black ink, brad and thread.

Leaf
Use an everyday accent, such as
a mini tag, as a mask stencil.
Place it, paint around it, let the
paint dry and remove.

Supplies *Mini tag:* Office Depot; *Acrylic
paint:* Delta Creative; *Stamps:* Hero Arts;
Other: Thread, brads and ribbon.

Paradise
Trace around a stencil mask with white
pen on colored cardstock.

Supplies *Stencil mask:* Heidi Swapp for
Advantus; *Wooden word:* Li'l Davis Designs;
White pen: Sharpie, Sanford; *Letter tabs:*
Making Memories; *Other:* Staples, thread
and torn notebook paper.

Friend
Stamp with masking fluid and ink around it. Let the ink dry, then remove masking fluid with your finger.

Supplies *Masking fluid:* Frisket Mask Fluid, Dr. Ph. Martin's; *Patterned papers:* Chatterbox and KI Memories; *Tab sticker:* Daisy D's Paper Co.; *Epoxy butterfly accent:* Autumn Leaves; *Stamps:* Hero Arts; *Other:* Ribbon, needle, safety pin, thread and tag.

Give Thanks
Punch shapes from cardstock to create your own stencil mask, then ink around it.

Supplies *Paper punches:* EK Success; *Stamps:* Hero Arts; *Stamping ink:* Tim Holtz Distress Ink, Ranger Industries; *Paper flower:* Prima; *Other:* Thread, staples and vintage paper.

Create
Doodle with a specialty masking pen and watercolor over it. Let dry, then remove masking fluid with your finger.*

Supplies *Liquid masking pen:* Masquepen; *Watercolor:* Hero Arts; *Patterned paper:* Creative Imaginations; *Plastic letters:* Heidi Swapp for Advantus; *Rub-ons and metal charm:* Making Memories; *"Memories" rub-on:* Wordsworth; *Other:* Ribbon.

Sally
Place stencil mask behind paper and sand over it to reveal the shape. ❤

Supplies *Letter stencil mask:* Heidi Swapp for Advantus; *Patterned papers and rub-ons:* KI Memories; *Paper flowers:* Prima; *Gems:* Hero Arts; *Other:* Thread.

* Achieve a similar effect without a masking pen by cutting out doodled shapes, placing them on cardstock and water coloring over.

tool time

brass stencils

stencil this in! | by JENNIFER MCGUIRE

Brass stencils courtesy of American Traditional Designs, The Stencil Collection and Lasting Impressions for Paper

For this Tool Time, I tried something new to me: brass stencils. I was amazed at the number of looks I could create with these versatile tools. They're so cool! You can dry emboss with them, trace them with markers or press them into clay. Whatever you do, I'm sure you'll love the results. Check out the 12 ideas I came up with!

Create playful patterned paper by doodling through stencils.

Mr. Personality. There is no better name for Cooper. This boy is full of personality. His silly expressions, funny sayings and priceless poses... they all contribute to his uncanny ability to win the heart of anyone. And to top it off, he is a good kid. Can't beat that.

Age 3
January 2006

Create a colorful card by applying clear ink over a stencil and rubbing with chalk.

Happy Spring

Create subtle accents for a background by stamping with clear ink and dry embossing.

• BOILING POOLS OF MUD THAT MADE US GIGGLE.

• WHETHER IT IS UNUSUAL, SIMPLY BEAUTIFUL OR JUST PLAIN BREATHTAKING, NEW ZEALAND IS FULL OF MANY OF GOD'S MOST AMAZING CREATIONS.

• COLORFUL FLOWERS THAT CAPTURE ATTENTION.

• HOT MINERAL POOLS THAT AMAZE THE EYES.

• VIVID GREEN FLORA EVERY WHICH WAY YOU TURN.

New Zealand

three great sources

American Traditional Designs
www.americantraditional.com

Lasting Impressions for Paper
www.lastingimpressions.com

The Stencil Collection
www.thestencilcollection.com

Mr. Personality by Jennifer McGuire. **Supplies** Brass stencils: The Stencil Collection (swirls and letters) and Lasting Impressions for Paper (stars and circles); Patterned paper: Chatterbox; Markers and letter stickers: American Crafts; Metal and plastic letters: Jo-Ann Scrap Essentials; Wood letters: Go West Studios; Computer font: CAC One Seventy, downloaded from the Internet; Other: Photo turns, ribbon and brads. • **Happy Spring Card** by Jennifer McGuire. **Supplies** Textured cardstock: Bazzill Basics Paper; Brass stencil: Stencilability, American Traditional Designs; Chalk: Craf-T Products; Other: Tag and thread. • **New Zealand** by Jennifer McGuire. **Supplies** Textured cardstock: Bazzill Basics Paper; Ribbon: May Arts and Creative Impressions; Stamping ink: VersaMark, Tsukineko; Brad: Making Memories; "Happy Spring" rubber stamp: Hero Arts; Computer font: AL Highlight, "15 Essential Fonts" CD, Autumn Leaves; Other: Vintage book paper and thread. Gems: Hero Arts; Rub-ons: Making Memories; Stamping ink: VersaMark, Tsukineko; Rub-ons: Making Memories; Stampabilities (large fern); Stamping ink: VersaMark, Tsukineko. Brass stencils: The Stencil Collection (small fern and dots) and Stampabilities (large fern).

Have Faith
Stamp firmly and repeatedly
over a positioned stencil.

Supplies *Patterned paper:* Wild Asparagus; *Brass stencil:*
American Traditional Designs; *Letter pieces:* foof-a-La,
Autumn Leaves; *Stamping ink:* VersaColor, Tsukineko;
Photo corners: K&Company; *Rubber stamp:* Hero Arts.

Love Me Tender
Rub through a stencil image onto
patterned paper or white-core
cardstock with sandpaper.

Supplies *Patterned papers:* KI Memories, K & Company
and foof-a-La, Autumn Leaves; *Brass stencil:* American
Traditional Designs; *Metal accent:* Go West Studios;
Ribbon: May Arts; *Corner-rounder punch:* EK Success;
Other: Thread and hatpin.

Miracle
Dry emboss through thin,
adhesive-backed metal and add
a jewel inside each design.

Supplies *Textured cardstock:* Bazzill Basics Paper; *Brass
stencil:* The Stencil Collection; *Sticker:* Making Memories;
Flower accent: KI Memories; *Gems:* Hero Arts; *Adhesive-
backed metal:* Duck, Henkel Consumer Adhesives; *Other:*
Ribbon, thread and scallop-edge scissors.

Simplify
Create a resist image on glossy paper,
then rub with dye-based ink.

Supplies *Brass stencil:* Lasting Impressions for
Paper; *Stamping ink:* Ranger Industries; *Buttons:*
foof-a-La, Autumn Leaves; *Ribbon:* May Arts;
Other: Thread and glossy white paper.

Special Delivery
Apply paste over a stencil image for added texture.

Supplies *Brass stencil:* American Traditional Designs; *Tags:* foof-a-La, Autumn Leaves; *Paste:* The Stencil Collection; *Ribbon:* May Arts; *Other:* Thread and charms.

Cherish Today
Press pigment ink over a stencil image, then heat emboss.

Supplies *Textured cardstock:* Bazzill Basics Paper; *Brass stencils:* Stampabilities; *Rubber stamps and embossing powder:* Hero Arts; *Stamping ink:* VersaMark, Tsukineko; Memories, Stewart Superior Corporation; Hero Arts; *Flower:* Prima; *Other:* Brads, thread, photo turn, photo corner, string and tag.

Friends
Use brass stencils as embellishments. Heat emboss them to alter the color. ♥

Cherish
Use stencil as a pattern to punch holes for hand-stitching.

Supplies *Textured cardstock:* Bazzill Basics Paper; *Brass stencil:* Lasting Impressions for Paper; *Rub-ons:* Autumn Leaves; *Sequins:* Doodlebug Design; *Flowers:* Prima; *Gem:* Hero Arts; *Computer font:* Century Gothic, Microsoft Word; *Other:* Brads, thread and button.

Supplies *Textured cardstock:* Bazzill Basics Paper; *Brass stencils:* Lasting Impressions for Paper; *Rubber stamps and embossing powder:* Hero Arts; *Rub-ons:* Doodlebug Design; *Ribbon:* May Arts; *Stamping ink:* VersaMark, Tsukineko; *Other:* Button, thread and brad.

tool time

die-cut machines

Dies courtesy of
Ellison, QuicKutz and Sizzix

designs to die for! | by JENNIFER MCGUIRE

Next time you're wishing for a versatile tool, think die-cut machines! They can be used for so much more than cutting simple accents straight from cardstock. Experiment with materials other than paper. Use the cutout shapes as patterns for other techniques. Think it. Dream it. Make it! Here are 12 ideas to get you started.

Die-cut metal sheets to create different accent shapes for a fun border. Simplify the process by using adhesive-backed metal.

Die-cut handmade paper or crumpled cardstock for the popular paper flower look!

Die-cut fabric for beautiful accents. While this is hard with scissors and impossible with punches, it's easy with a die-cut machine!

Home to Me by Jennifer McGuire. **Supplies** Die cuts: QuicKutz (title, photo corner and round tag) and Sizzix (heart, spiral border, tags, bookplate and photo turns); Adhesive-backed metal: Duck, Henkel Consumer Adhesives; Buttons: Buttons Galore; Brads and jelly embellishments: Making Memories; Rubber stamps: Hero Arts; Stamping ink: StazOn, Tsukineko; Woven label: me & my BIG ideas; Acrylic and metal circles: KI Memories. • **Treasure** by Jennifer McGuire. **Supplies** Patterned paper: Anna Griffin; Die cuts: Sizzix (flowers) and QuicKutz (photo corner); Fabric: Hobby Lobby; Computer font: DisProporz, downloaded from the Internet; Other: Buttons and thread. • **Paper Flower Card** by Jennifer McGuire. **Supplies** Textured paper: Creative Imaginations; Patterned papers: Paper Adventures; Die cuts: Sizzix; Gems: Hero Arts and Making Memories; Metal accents: K&Company; Other: Photo corners.

Bliss
Create transparent shapes.

Supplies *Transparency:* Creative Imaginations; *Die cuts:* Sizzix; *Rubber stamps:* Hero Arts; *Stamping ink:* Ranger Industries; *Fabric tag:* K&Company; *Ribbon:* May Arts; *Other:* Paint swatch and brads.

Envelope
Die-cut foam, then adhere it to plastic to create quick and easy foam stamps.

Supplies *Patterned papers:* Making Memories and me & my BIG ideas; *Die cut:* Sizzix; *Button:* SEI; *Acrylic paint:* Delta Creative; *Computer font:* AL Updated Classic, "15 Essential Fonts" CD, Autumn Leaves; *Other:* Foam, ribbon, paper clips, string and thread.

Sunshine
Put a bottle cap between the plastic pieces of the die-cut machine and flatten the cap with one quick pass. *Note:* Apply pressure with care so you don't damage your machine.

Supplies *Patterned paper:* Die Cuts With a View; *Die cut:* Sizzix; *Bottle cap:* Mustard Moon; *Rub-ons:* Wordsworth ("you are my" and "sunshine") and Autumn Leaves ("SUNSHINE"); *Sequins:* Doodlebug Design; *Computer font:* AL Updated Classic, "15 Essential Fonts" CD, Autumn Leaves; *Other:* Thread, brads and transparency. Photograph by Cindy Traidman.

Luv U
Use the "negative" shape from the die-cut cardstock as a stencil for inking.

Supplies *Patterned papers, lace and hatpin:* Making Memories; *Die cuts:* Sizzix (letters) and QuicKutz (heart); *Flower:* Prima; *Brad:* Making Memories; *Rubber stamps:* Hero Arts; *Stamping ink:* VersaColor, Tsukineko; *Other:* Thread.

School Pictures
Make your own "sequins"
from thin sheets of plastic.

Supplies *Chipboard letter:* Making Memories; *Rub-ons and round sequins:* Doodlebug Design; *Die cut:* Ellison; *Thin plastic:* Office Depot (from file folders) and Ranger Industries; *Other:* Ribbon and thread.

XOXO
Use negative letter shapes for
a unique title.

Supplies *Die cuts:* Sizzix; *Acrylic heart:* Heidi Grace Designs; *Jewel brads:* Magic Scraps; *Other:* Patterned paper, wire and thread.

Audrey
Die-cut shrink-film paper,
then heat the letters
for mini accents! ❤

Supplies *Metal-rimmed tag:* Making Memories; *Die cuts:* Sizzix; *Shrink film:* Grafix; *Buttons:* SEI; *Fabric:* Jo-Ann Scrap Essentials; *Stencil:* Office Depot; *Other:* Thread.

Together
Cover paper with adhesive and lay
ribbon over it, then die-cut to
create ribbon-covered shapes.

Supplies *Die cuts:* Sizzix; *Hatpin and charm:* Making Memories; *Woven label:* Jo-Ann Scrap Essentials; *Other:* Ribbon.

tools & techniques

{ brads }

This was one of Colin's first gifts on the day he was born: a stuffed monkey from Uncle Mike. When Colin first got it, he was about the same size as the monkey. Now, the monkey gets tossed around the floor as they play. This is one gift we will be sure to keep. Good memories. 10/06

create JOY

gift

fasten tight | by JENNIFER MCGUIRE

Brads are a must-have for any scrapbooker. They're perfect for attaching vellum, transparencies and other papers to your pages. But brads can be used for so much more! Here are 10 ideas I came up with. Have fun, get creative and see what you can do, too. >

Gift by Jennifer McGuire. Photos by Angela Talentino of Essenza Studio, Cincinnati. **Supplies** *Brads:* Autumn Leaves (rhinestone and silver rimmed) and Making Memories (others); *Cardstock:* Bazzill Basics Paper; *Patterned paper:* Anna Griffin; *Die-cut hearts and letters:* Cricut, Provo Craft.

quick & hip

Create a spot for hidden journaling behind a photo. Attach with a brad, allowing the photo to swing open.

Best Gift *by Jennifer McGuire.* **Supplies** *Brad:* Autumn Leaves; *Star gems:* KI Memories; *Font:* CK Odd Ball, downloaded from *www.scrapnfonts.com; Other:* Staples and metal-rimmed tag.

Attach charms with small brads. Let charms hang loose, or hammer the top lightly to keep charms in place.

Cherish *by Jennifer McGuire.* **Supplies** *Brads:* Queen & Co. (small) and Bazzill Basics Paper (heart); *Charms:* Blue Moon Beads (ovals), Making Memories ("cherish") and Frost Creek Charms (all others); *Trim:* Making Memories.

Create bullet points with dimension!

Eight Reasons *by Jennifer McGuire.* **Supplies** *Brads:* Queen & Co.; *Patterned papers:* Autumn Leaves (blue), Chatterbox (yellow) and FontWerks (green); *Wood number:* Li'l Davis Designs; *Fonts:* Mank Sans (title) and Ocelot Monowidth (list), downloaded from the Internet; *Other:* Ribbon and thread.

Give stamped, rub-on or sticker images a bit of dimension and added color.

Spring *by Jennifer McGuire.* **Supplies** *Brads:* Accent Depot; *Stamps and embossing powder:* Hero Arts; *Ink:* VersaMark, Tsukineko; *Ribbon:* SEI; *Other:* Thread.

Sand the paint from brads for a worn look.

Taylor *by Jennifer McGuire.* **Supplies** *Brads:* Making Memories; *Patterned paper and letter stickers:* KI Memories; *Other:* Sandpaper and thread.

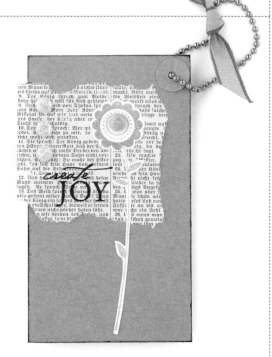

Dip in liquid adhesive and sprinkle glitter on top for a sparkly look.

Create Joy *by Jennifer McGuire.* **Supplies** *Brads:* Creative Impressions; *Stamps and glitter:* Hero Arts; *Ink:* VersaColor, Tsukineko; *Liquid adhesive:* Diamond Glaze, JudiKins; *Ribbon:* American Crafts; *Other:* Beaded chain and vintage paper.

Hold pleated ribbon in place.

Heart *by Jennifer McGuire.* **Supplies** *Brad:* Making Memories; *Patterned papers:* Anna Griffin (green) and FontWerks (orange); *Die-cut heart:* My Mind's Eye; *Ribbon:* Pebbles Inc.; *Other:* Doily and thread.

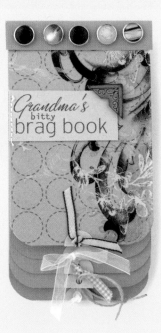

Bind several tags together for a make-it-yourself tag book.

Brag Book *by Jennifer McGuire.* **Supplies** *Brads:* Autumn Leaves; *Patterned paper:* SEI; *Printed transparency:* Autumn Leaves; *Ribbon:* May Arts; *Photo corner:* Daisy D's Paper Co.; *Fonts:* Holiday House and Interstate, downloaded from the Internet; *Other:* Jute and thread.

Kay *by Jennifer McGuire.*
Supplies *Brads:* Autumn Leaves; *Sequins:* Queen & Co.; *Paper and glitter stickers:* Making Memories; *Font:* TypoSlabserif-Light, downloaded from the Internet; *Other:* Jute, acetate flower, thread and beads.

Create unique envelope closures with these easy steps:

1 Insert brad through acetate flower, then tie twine around the back side of the brad. (The flower should be between the twine and the front of the brad.)

2 Insert brad through envelope, below the flap.

3 Insert a second brad through another acetate flower and secure it through the envelope's flap.

4 Wrap twine around brads (below the flowers) to secure the envelope closed.

try it yourself!

Ready to try these simple techniques? Check out the brad selection from these manufacturers:

• Accent Depot
www.paperwishes.com

• Autumn Leaves
www.autumnleaves.com

• Making Memories
www.makingmemories.com

• Queen & Co.
www.queenandco.com ♥

tools & techniques

Spice up buttons by attaching them with a variety of goodies, including ribbon, rickrack, torn fabric, jute, floral wire and string.

I have met some great people through scrapbooking. A good example? Lisa Russo. This girl is a true gem. Several years ago, I was working on putting a team together for Designing with Words. Because I was a huge fan of her work, I contacted Lisa. Thankfully, she said yes. We instantly became friends. Over the years, she has been so good to work with, so fun to laugh with and simply perfect to chat with. I just love her to pieces. So, when Ken and my doctor recommended I get away for a girls weekend, I knew just where to head for the perfect carefree weekend. Lisa was a lovely hostess and had everything planned so thoughtfully. (A Lisa trademark!) We chatted and chatted and chatted some more. A real treat. In addition, one of the best things about visiting Lisa was meeting her kiddos. They are gems, just like their mom. I loved getting to spend time with Aidan and Ava, since I know so much about them. Those kids are so fortunate to have Lisa as a mom. Just like I am fortunate to have her as a friend. (08/06)

button frenzy | by JENNIFER MCGUIRE

ONE OF MY FAVORITE treasures from my dear grandma is her box of old buttons. I've held onto them for years. When I started scrapbooking, I decided to use them on my pages—and I quickly became addicted. I use buttons on almost every page now! Buttons can be used in so many creative ways—here are a few to try. ›

Fortunate by Jennifer McGuire. Photo by Victor Russo. **Supplies** *Buttons:* Autumn Leaves; *Cardstock:* Bazzill Basics Paper; *Paper flower:* Prima; *Letter die cuts:* Cricut, Provo Craft; *Ribbon:* Making Memories; *Font:* Blue Highway Condensed, downloaded from the Internet; *Other:* Rickrack, string, fabric, floral wire and jute.

four fast ideas

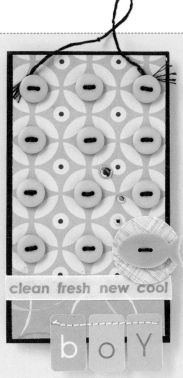

Add dimension to flat paper by incorporating buttons into the pattern.

Boy *by Jennifer McGuire.* **Supplies** *Buttons:* SEI (blue) and Making Memories (fish); *Patterned papers:* Close To My Heart (blue) and Paperfever (green); *Ribbon and letter stickers:* KI Memories; *Gems:* Hero Arts; *Embroidery floss:* DMC; *Other:* Thread.

Stamp a title or image onto plain buttons. Use permanent stamping ink and adhere the button to the layout first so it won't stick to the inked stamp.

Be Mine *by Jennifer McGuire.* **Supplies** *Clear buttons and stamps:* Hero Arts; *Textured paper:* Fibermark; *Patterned paper:* Chatterbox; *Trim, ribbon and clip:* Making Memories; *Rub-ons:* 7gypsies; *Stamping ink:* StazOn, Tsukineko; *Other:* Thread.

Create one-of-a-kind accents by adhering patterned papers or photos behind clear buttons. Use a clear-drying glue stick for best results.

100% Fascinated *by Jennifer McGuire.* **Supplies** *Buttons:* Autumn Leaves (round), Doodlebug Design (flower) and Stampin' Up! (round); *Patterned papers:* Anna Griffin (red), Chatterbox (stripe), KI Memories (orange), Scenic Route (dot asterisk) and SEI (pink); *Ribbon:* C.M. Offray & Son; *Fonts:* CK Frankfurt, www.scrapnfonts.com; Interstate, downloaded from the Internet; *Other:* Faux flower and thread.

Add interest simply by layering buttons and tying them together with thread.

Life *by Jennifer McGuire.* **Supplies** *Buttons:* Buttons Galore (shell), Hero Arts (small green and small heart), Autumn Leaves (stars and square), Crystalline Crafts (small white), Hot Off The Press (teal and green), SEI (orange and tan), Doodlebug Design (house and large heart) and Stampin' Up! (rounded square); *Patterned papers:* Autumn Leaves; *Textured paper:* Creative Imaginations; *Stamps:* Hero Arts; *Stamping ink:* Ranger Industries; *Other:* Thread.

four ideas for play

Use buttons as stamps. Temporarily adhere a button to an acrylic block (or anything else solid). Then ink and stamp!

McGuires by Jennifer McGuire. **Supplies** Buttons (used as stamps): Hero Arts; Stamping ink: VersaColor, Tsukineko; Patterned papers: KI Memories (orange) and SEI (pink); Chipboard letter and letter stickers: Making Memories; Velvet flower sticker: SEI; Other: Brad.

Create your own buttons by punching two or four small "buttonholes" in circle (or shaped!) epoxies, punched papers or chipboard shapes—tie string or ribbon in the holes. It's easiest to punch holes if you temporarily adhere the accents to scrap paper first.

One Month by Jennifer McGuire. **Supplies** Epoxy accents (punched into circles): MOD, Autumn Leaves; Textured paper: Fibermark; Chipboard stars: Heidi Swapp for Advantus; Other: Tag, ribbon, stamping ink, pen and thread.

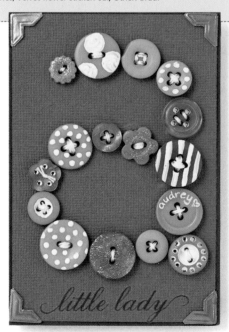

Add custom patterns to plain buttons with paint, paint pens or gems.

Little Lady by Jennifer McGuire. **Supplies** Buttons: Autumn Leaves, Buttons Galore and Doodlebug Design; Gems: Hero Arts; Paint: Delta Creative; White pen: Sharpie, Sanford; Rub-ons: Die Cuts With a View; Other: String and photo corners.

Create your own mini-book closures by wrapping string around two buttons (one attached on each flap).

Zoo by Jennifer McGuire. **Supplies** Buttons and letter sticker: Doodlebug Design; Patterned paper: Déjà Views by The C-Thru Ruler Co.; Ribbon: Pebbles Inc.; Rub-ons: BasicGrey; Font: Ocelot Monowidth, downloaded from the Internet; Other: String.

Sweet Sunshine
by Jennifer McGuire.
Supplies *Buttons:* Stampin'
Up!; *Patterned paper:*
Scenic Route; *Chipboard
word ("sunshine"):* Li'l Davis
Designs; *Epoxy accent
("sweet"):* Sue Dreamer,
Colorbök; *Circle die cut:*
Cricut, Provo Craft; *Other:*
Fabric and string.

Give your buttons a soft look by adding fabric. Simply follow these easy steps:

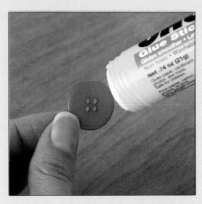

1 Generously apply glue stick to the top of a button and adhere to the wrong side of fabric.

2 Turn the button upside down and cut the fabric along the button's edge.

3 Fray the edges of the fabric by gently scratching them with your fingernail. This adds a home-made look.

try it yourself!

Ready to start playing with buttons? Check out options from these manufacturers:

• Buttons Galore and More
www.morebuttons.com

• foof-a-La, Autumn Leaves
www.autumnleaves.com

• Doodlebug Design
www.doodlebug.ws

• Hot Off The Press
www.paperwishes.com

Like the look of buttons but don't want the added bulk? Try button-shaped brads from Hot Off the Press and The Eyelet Outlet, or look for button-shaped epoxies from The Beary Patch. ♥

tools & techniques { sequins }

a little bling | by JENNIFER MCGUIRE

I REMEMBER playing with sequins as a kid. I used them to decorate any *and all* of my craft-project creations. It's no different now! I still love sequins and how they can add a bit of fun to any page. Check out these ideas for your sequin satisfaction. ›

oh so easy

Bring stamped images to life by embellishing them with sequins.

Truly Blessed *by Jennifer McGuire.* **Supplies** *Sequins:* Queen & Co. (orange and white) and Cartwright's (yellow); *Chipboard tag:* Gin-X, Imagination Project; *Gems and rubber stamp:* Hero Arts; *Sticker ("truly blessed"):* Wordsworth; *Other:* Thread, staples and jute.

Add pizzazz to titles by dotting an "i" or replacing an "o" with a sequin.

My Smilin' Colin *by Jennifer McGuire.* **Supplies** *Sequins:* Doodlebug Design; *Tag:* 7gypsies; *Patterned paper:* KI Memories; *Chipboard letters:* Heidi Swapp for Advantus.

Back a plain brad with a sequin for added interest.

Love *by Jennifer McGuire.* **Supplies** *Sequins and stamp:* Hero Arts; *Patterned paper:* Autumn Leaves; *Textured paper:* FiberMark; *Ink:* ColorBox, Clearsnap; *Brads:* Making Memories; *Other:* Thread and string.

Tie sequins onto string and dangle from chipboard accents.

Twinkle *by Jennifer McGuire.* **Supplies** *Sequins:* Cartwright's; *Cardstock:* Prism Papers; *Patterned paper:* cherryArte; *Ribbon:* KI Memories; *Chipboard star:* Gin-X, Imagination Project; *Letter stickers:* Making Memories; *Glitter paint:* Delta Creative; *Other:* Thread, string and vintage paper.

Use sequins to form a frame, drawing attention to a photo subject.

Little Guy *by Jennifer McGuire.* **Supplies** *Sequins:* Hero Arts; *Cardstock:* Bazzill Basics Paper; *Font:* Copperplate Gothic Light, downloaded from the Internet.

Arrange sequins along an edge to form a decorative border.

Love *by Jennifer McGuire.* **Supplies** *Sequins and rickrack:* Doodlebug Design; *Ribbon:* KI Memories; *Rub-ons:* BasicGrey (white) and Déjà Views by The C-Thru Ruler Co. (orange); *Button:* Autumn Leaves; *Other:* Envelope, tag, thread and fabric.

Apply glitter to sequins (before adhering to project) for added shimmer.

Sassy *by Jennifer McGuire.* **Supplies** *Sequins:* Westrim Crafts; *Patterned paper:* KI Memories; *Die-cut scalloped circle:* Cricut, Provo Craft; *Charm and beaded chain:* Making Memories; *Thread:* DMC; *Brads:* Karen Foster Design; *Ribbon:* Mrs. Grossman's; *Other:* Cardstock, thread and glitter.

Incorporate sequins into the design of patterned paper.

A *by Jennifer McGuire.* **Supplies** *Sequins:* Cartwright's; *Patterned paper:* SEI; *Epoxy stickers:* SEI (flower) and KI Memories ("a"); *Other:* Tag, thread and string.

proud

Sew sequins to a page for an unexpected look.

Proud *by Jennifer McGuire.*
Supplies *Sequins:* Doodlebug Design; *Cardstock:* Bazzill Basics Paper; *Glitter letter stickers:* Making Memories; *Font:* 2Peas Peachy Keen, downloaded from *www.twopeasinabucket.com; Thread:* Coats & Clark.

Anniversary *by Jennifer McGuire.* **Supplies** *Sequins:* Doodlebug Design; *Patterned paper:* 7gypsies (blue) and K&Company (tan); *Acrylic flower:* Queen & Co.; *Stamps:* Hero Arts; *Ink:* StazOn, Tsukineko; *Tag and gem brad:* Making Memories; *Other:* Ribbon and thread.

Stamp on sequins with these simple steps:

1 Lay sticky note on table with the sticky side up. Lay button in the sticky portion to temporarily hold in place. Position a sequin next to it.

2 Stamp on the sequin with permanent ink (I use StazOn by Tsukineko)—be sure to stamp quickly and lightly. The sticky note prevents the sequin from sticking to the wet stamp.

3 Let sequin dry completely and remove from sticky note.

Tip: Use these same steps to stamp on buttons. Step 1 also works great when preparing to add glitter to sequins.

try it yourself!

Ready to start playing with sequins? Check out options from these manufacturers:

• Doodlebug Design   • Hero Arts   • Queen & Co.   • Westrim Crafts ♥

Find links to these manufacturer websites at *www.creatingkeepsakes.com/juneproducts.*

ck hot
spot

by LORI FAIRBANKS

fancy flourishes

ORNAMENTAL SWIRLS AND FLOURISHES are super hot! You'll see them on everything from T-shirts to wrought-iron creations. They're popular for scrapbook pages as well!

Add artsy flair—fast—with rub-ons, stickers, rubber stamps and more. Enjoy this page by Jenni Bowlin, then use fancy flourishes to adorn your next page! ♥

Mix multiple types and sizes of decorative flourishes for a chic look. *Page by Jenni Bowlin.* **Supplies** *Patterned papers:* Autumn Leaves (red) and Melissa Frances (dot); *Rub-on swirl:* My Mind's Eye; *Clear plastic letters, chipboard arrow and fuzzy rub-on letters:* Heidi Swapp for Advantus; *Chipboard swirls:* Jenni Bowlin Studio; *Stamp:* Delta Creative; *Metallic paint:* Li'l Davis Designs; *Star sticker:* Avery; *Other:* Vintage crystals, pen and staples.

Consider ornamental flourishes from the following companies:

❶ Autumn Leaves
www.autumnleaves.com

❷ BasicGrey
www.basicgrey.com

❸ K&Company
www.kandcompany.com

❹ Making Memories
www.makingmemories.com

❺ Sandylion
www.sandylion.com

Timesaving Stickers

7 tips
for quick, easy, budget-friendly pages

Like many other little girls, I had a sticker collection. I loved buying special stickers, trading them with friends and organizing them in my sticker album. Fast forward 20 years, and I still love stickers. My tastes have changed a bit (I've moved on from scratch-and-sniff to acid free!), but I still have a huge collection. I've discovered that stickers are sensational for creating nice, quick and inexpensive scrapbook pages. >

by Lisa Brown Caveney

To help you see how versatile stickers are, I and three other scrapbookers created the following layouts using *only stickers and the basics: cardstock, photos, computer fonts and pens*. Each layout emphasizes a tip that's perfect for any budget-conscious scrapbooker on a tight schedule.

Want to know what we found most exciting? Each layout was created in *under an hour, cost less* than $5, and provided *plenty of leftover stickers for another project!*

Mix and Match Styles

No one ever said you have to use the same type of stickers on a layout. Mixing and matching sticker styles can be a lot of fun and add a creative twist.

I combined a photorealistic sticker with die-cut stickers to create this border. The ruler sticker also reinforces my layout's theme about hair length.

Time Spent: 45 minutes ✳ Cost: $4.75

Long to Short by *Lisa Brown Caveney*. **Supplies** *Flower stickers:* KI Memories; *Ruler sticker:* Nostalgiques, EK Success; *Pen:* Zig Writer, EK Success.

Use Different Sticker Themes

When selecting stickers for a layout, sometimes the perfect choice isn't the most apparent. On this layout, Carrie chose to use a flower sticker on a fall layout. It's just the right touch to make the layout feminine and visually mesh the color of the leaves with her daughter's blue outfit. Placing a brown cardstock circle behind Carrie's flower sticker makes it pop.

Time Spent: 45 minutes ✳ Cost: $3

Fresh Fall by Carrie Owens. **Supplies** *Textured cardstock:* Bazzill Basics Paper; *Pen:* Zig Millennium, EK Success; *Cardstock stickers:* KI Memories; *Title and journaling:* Carrie's own designs.

Sticker Strategy

The space on each scrapbook page is precious. Each time I add an element, I want it to serve a specific purpose. Remember, stickers are not just decorative—they can fill a design role as well. When using stickers, try to make sure they serve at least one of these functions:

- Reinforce your layout's message with shapes, patterns or themes.
- Complement the color scheme.
- Fill in empty or trapped space.

Note how the layouts in this article all incorporate one, two or all three of these design guidelines.

Trim Stickers with Scissors

Trimming stickers can be a great way to alter their look to fit your layout. I wanted clean, straight lines in this layout, and the large, round baseball stickers just weren't fitting in with my design scheme.

My solution was to mount the stickers on squares of gray cardstock and trim off the overhanging portion. This way, I could use the baseball stickers to highlight my theme while still maintaining the linear look I wanted.

Time Spent: 30 minutes * Cost: $2.50

ON JULY 2 DEREK AND I JOINED A BUNCH OF OUR FRIENDS TO WATCH THE OAKLAND A'S TAKE ON THE CHICAGO WHITE SOX. WE HAD A GREAT GROUP — ANNA AND GORDON, NATALIE AND ANDY, BETHANY AND TIM, PLUS ERIN AND ANDY TOOK THE BART FROM PLEASANTON, CRAIG AND CHRIS DROVE UP FROM THE SOUTH BAY AND PETE WAS VISITING FROM MN. THE A'S ENDED UP LOSING 3-5 BUT WE HAD A GREAT TIME AT THE GAME TOGETHER.

baseball

Baseball *by Lisa Brown Caveney.* **Supplies** *Stickers:* Sticko by EK Success; *Pen:* Zig Writer, EK Success.

New Ideas for Border Stickers

Border stickers can be used for so much more! Wendy trimmed down border stickers to outline her color-blocked background and frame the adorable photo of her little one. With muted earth tones, she effectively used several different patterned stickers without overpowering her layout.

Time Spent: 30 minutes   *   **Cost:** $3.25

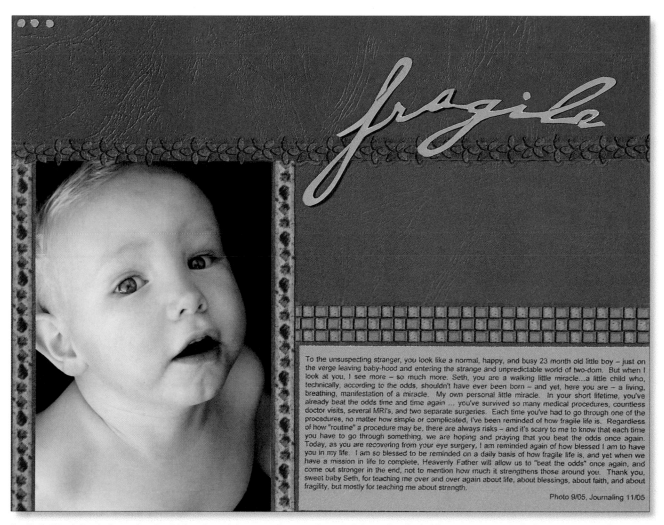

fragile

To the unsuspecting stranger, you look like a normal, happy, and busy 23 month old little boy – just on the verge leaving baby-hood and entering the strange and unpredictable world of two-dom. But when I look at you, I see more – so much more. Seth, you are a walking little miracle...a little child who, technically, according to the odds, shouldn't have ever been born – and yet, here you are – a living, breathing, manifestation of a miracle. My own personal little miracle. In your short lifetime, you've already beat the odds time and time again ... you've survived so many medical procedures, countless doctor visits, several MRI's, and two separate surgeries. Each time you've had to go through one of the procedures, no matter how simple or complicated, I've been reminded of how fragile life is. Regardless of how "routine" a procedure may be, there are always risks – and it's scary to me to know that each time you have to go through something, we are hoping and praying that you beat the odds once again. Today, as you are recovering from your eye surgery, I am reminded again of how blessed I am to have you in my life. I am so blessed to be reminded on a daily basis of how fragile life is, and yet when we have a mission in life to complete, Heavenly Father will allow us to "beat the odds" once again, and come out stronger in the end, not to mention how much it strengthens those around you. Thank you, sweet baby Seth, for teaching me over and over again about life, about blessings, about faith, and about fragility, but mostly for teaching me about strength.

Photo 9/05, Journaling 11/05

Fragile *by Wendy Sue Anderson.* **Supplies** *Stickers:* Paper Adventures; *Computer fonts:* AL Cadence, downloaded from www.twopeasinabucket.com; Guatami, downloaded from the Internet.

Create a Sticker Collage

Making a mosaic using several stickers is an easy way to make a large accent. I tiled six key stickers together to balance out the photos on the left side of my layout and mirror my key theme.

With such busy photos and a strong accent, I kept things from getting too overwhelming by using a muted color palette.

Time Spent: 20 minutes ✳ Cost: $2.25

Keys to My Heart by Lisa Brown Caveney. **Supplies** Stickers: Nostalgiques, EK Success; Pen: Zig Writer, EK Success.

Accessorize Handmade Accents

Stickers are a great way to dress up cardstock die cuts or hand-cut embellishments. Bonnie hand-cut flower accents and topped them off with round stickers for centers. Arranging the flower accents at an angle allowed space for a large photo, a title and accents, without making the layout seem cramped.

Time Spent: 45 minutes ✳ Cost: $2.75

Hip Huggers *by Bonnie Lotz.* **Supplies** *Stickers:* Carolee's Creations; *Computer font:* CK Easy Goin', "Super Combo Bonus Font" CD, *Creating Keepsakes.*

Repurpose "Remnant" Stickers

Square stickers really are versatile. One of my favorite ways to use them is to snip them in half diagonally and use them as photo corners. I created this border with stickers that were around the perimeter of a sheet of letter stickers.

Although the clear border stickers looked great on the white backing sheet, they lost their color when I placed them over the orange cardstock and photos in my layout. To solve this problem, I mounted the stickers on thin strips of white cardstock before attaching them to my page.

Time Spent: 45 minutes ✴ Cost: $3.50

Anniversary *by Lisa Brown Caveney.* **Supplies** *Square stickers:* Mrs. Grossman's; *Border stickers:* Kathy Davis; *Pen:* Zig Writer, EK Success.

Surplus Solutions

Every scrapbooker has them—those half-used sticker sheets you just don't know how to use. Beyond adorning scrapbook pages, stickers stick to just about anything. So, brush off the dust and put those oldies to good use!

• Create cards with sticker embellishments.

• Seal envelopes with a sticker.

• Mount stickers on magnetic backing sheets to make refrigerator magnets.

• Donate stickers to an elementary school or any program that needs art supplies.

• Give your kids stickers as special treats or to scrapbook along with you.

• Embellish gift tags or store-bought gift bags with stickers. ❤

USE THOSE

SCRAPS!

TRY YOUR HAND AT PAPER PIECING

I LOVE PAPER. *Patterned. Cardstock. Textured.* It all finds its way into my scrapbook stash, where I end up with more than my share of scraps. I can't bear to toss any into the trashcan, so I squirrel them away in my scrap box.

The best part? My scraps don't collect dust. I use them, big and small, to create paper-pieced designs for my scrapbook pages. Funky flowers are a favorite—they're fun and they don't have to be "perfect" (how's that for a nice twist?). Here's how I paper-pieced different flower looks.

I also asked three scrapbookers to rummage through their scraps and come up with paper-pieced designs of their own. You'll love their creations!

BY MARIE COX

Abstract flowers add a funky touch to pages, and creating them is as simple as cutting scraps into "primitive" triangles and arranging them around a circle. Don't worry about making the pieces perfectly symmetrical or the same size—the imperfection adds to the artistic feel.

Do not let others define you, you can be whatever you want. Reach as high and far as you can because you only live this life once and there are no second chances. Know that you are beautiful and brilliant and yes, those two things can go together. You are all that I am, all that I had hoped to be.

LISTEN

Listen by Marie Cox. **Supplies** Textured cardstock: Bazzill Basics Paper and Die Cuts With a View; Buttons: Junkitz; Rub-on letters: Studio K, K&Company; Computer font: Headline, downloaded from the Internet.

» more flower ideas

Want to create other cool blooms? Try the following:

• Overlap abstract circles.
• Arrange hand-cut petals around a button.
• Mix and match patterned papers and cardstock.
• Play with fun mixed-media items.

mixing patterned papers

Choosing patterned papers that work well together doesn't have to be difficult. Just follow these guidelines:

❶ Use papers from the same manufacturer. Many paper lines feature coordinating designs that are meant to be used together. Take advantage of the designers' knowledge!

❷ Select papers that feature the same color within the patterns. It's easy to combine a variety of patterns effectively if they have a color in common.

❸ Consider the scale of the patterns you choose. Small patterns work well with other small patterns, while large patterns work well with other large patterns.

Blue Flower *by Marie Cox.* **Supplies** *Textured cardstock:* Bazzill Basics Paper; *Metal sheet:* Making Memories; *Patterned paper:* Scrapworks.

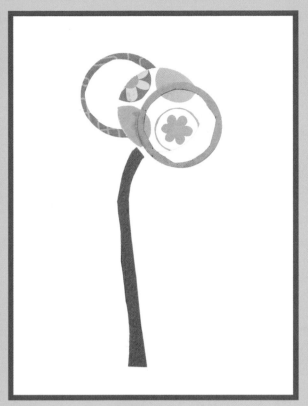

Pink Flower *by Marie Cox.* **Supplies** *Textured cardstock:* Bazzill Basics Paper, *Patterned papers:* KI Memories and Paperfever.

Green Flower *by Marie Cox.* **Supplies** *Textured cardstock:* Die Cuts With a View; *Button:* Junkitz.

Brown Flower *by Marie Cox.* **Supplies** *Textured cardstock:* Bazzill Basics Paper; *Patterned paper:* Anna Griffin; *Button:* 7gypsies; *Stamping ink:* ColorBox Fluid Chalk, Clearsnap.

3 twists from scrapbookers

I asked Jamie Waters, Jennifer McGuire and Bonnie Lotz to dig out their scraps and create their own paper-pieced accents. Here's what they came up with!

«

Full-Page
Flower
Accent

Life Is Good *by Jamie Waters.* **Supplies** *Patterned papers:* KI Memories and American Crafts; *Label stickers:* K&Company; *Rub-on stitching:* Fontwerks.

jamie's notes:

I love digging through my scrap box and finding colors and patterns that work together. To create the paper-pieced flower on my page, I chose patterns from my favorite paper lines that looked good together. I kept the flower shape simple and left a lot of white space in the background so my design wouldn't look busy.

Boy? Girl? Blue? Pink?

We don't know.

Everyone asks and we often wonder.

But, not knowing has been a good thing for us and our wallets. We haven't been able to buy clothes for the little one just yet.

Perfect

In fact, we own one shirt now. It works great for a boy or girl, and comes from our favorite store, Baby Gap.

It simply says "perfect" in silver. After all, regardless if the baby is a boy or girl, the baby will be just perfect for us.

photo taken December, 2005
(note the big 29-week belly)

Perfect *by Jennifer McGuire.* **Supplies** *Patterned papers:* KI Memories, Paperfever, Chatterbox, Daisy D's Paper Co. and Making Memories; *Letter stickers:* American Crafts; *Button:* Doodlebug Design; *Punch:* EK Success; *Computer font:* McBooHmk, "Scrapbook Studio" CD, Hallmark.

jennifer's notes:

When I can't find the perfect embellishment, I often turn to my scraps. I like to keep my paper-pieced designs subtle, using basic patterns like flowers or hearts. Here, I decided to combine the two in a paisley pattern.

I drew the outline of a few paisley shapes on the back of some patterned-paper scraps. (If you prefer, print a clip-art image on the back of the paper instead.) I cut the paisley shapes out, leaving just the outline, and filled them with a mix of hearts, circles and flower pieces from random patterned papers. The result is a stylish but subtle background for my page.

VARIATION: I like to keep scraps of wrapping paper with fun flowers and other patterns on hand. They're great inspiration for paper-pieced designs!

>> Graphic Heart Accent

Lets take a smile! I remember your cute little two year old self saying this many times. I guess I had you trained really early. With such a cute and willing subject I am always ready to take a smile.

Miquelle age 8

treasure adore

Miquelle *by Bonnie Lotz.* **Supplies** *Patterned papers:* Provo Craft (yellow flowers, red swirl, cream speckles and pink swirl), EK Success (buttons), Lasting Impressions for Paper (red dot), Chatterbox (red flowers), Die Cuts With a View (brown dot), Karen Foster Design (red speckle) and Creative Imaginations (pink words); *Rub-on letters:* Doodlebug Design; *Computer font:* CK Newsprint, "Fresh Fonts" CD, *Creating Keepsakes*; *Other:* Photo turn.

bonnie's notes:

I can't throw scraps away—even the tiniest pieces—so it feels great to put them to good use! For this page, I cut my patterned papers and cardstock pieces into strips. I traced the heart shape onto my page, then began building by starting at the inside and working outward, trimming the strips to the right length. I found it easier to glue the pieces down as I went rather than wait until I had them all in place.

VARIATION: For a fun paper-piecing alternative, punch shapes (like circles or squares) from patterned paper and use them as accents. ❤

On the escalator out of the

Metro, Smithsonian station.

linked together

I love that when you go out

into the world together

you hold hands.

Exploring Washington D.C.

March 2006

chain link charm

EXAGGERATED CHAIN LINKS are all the rage, from traditional metal ovals to opaque plastic finishes in circles and irregularly bent shapes. A popular twist combines different link sizes and finishes. Check out this page by Tracy Miller, then use chain-linked accents in paper or metal on your next page. ♥

Use patterned paper with strong circular designs to cut out paper rings to link together. *Page by Tracy Miller.* **Supplies** *Patterned paper and letter stickers:* American Crafts; *Letter and heart stickers:* Doodlebug Design; *Computer font:* Tahoma, Microsoft Word.

Use a circle cutter to cut rings from patterned paper or cardstock. Consider items from the following companies:

❶ Fiskars
www.fiskarscrafts.com

❷ Creative Memories
www.creativememories.com

❸ Making Memories
www.makingmemories.com

❹ Provo Craft
www.provocraft.com

get more from your PUNCHES

I'M A SUCKER FOR NEW CLOTHES. Lately, not only have the clothes been new, they've been a little on the expensive side. How do I justify the purchases when my hubby sees the receipts? I use the cost-per-wear rule! If I wear a more expensive item enough times that the cost per wear is only a few dollars, then I consider the purchase a sound investment.

The same rule goes for the punches lingering in my scrap stash. They cost a lot, and after I considered that I'd only used each on a few layouts, I knew I needed to bring new life to my stash. If you're in the same situation, break out those punches. I've got plenty of ways to bring your cost per use down to pennies!

To start, I used one technique for placing punches perfectly and another for stitching accents. Three members of the CK team tried the techniques as well, adding their own twists. Read on to see how each of our projects turned out!

by erin lincoln

About the Author

Erin has scrapbooked for five and a half years. She keeps a list of to-do topics, and whenever she thinks of a new way to use a product, she checks the list to see if she can find a perfect match. Rather than scrapbooking chronologically, Erin "goes with the flow and what feels right," producing results she calls "interesting." Erin and her husband, Matt, live in Maryland.

Perfect Placement

Do you find it difficult to line punches up correctly on a page? Relax!
You can create simple guides in three steps:

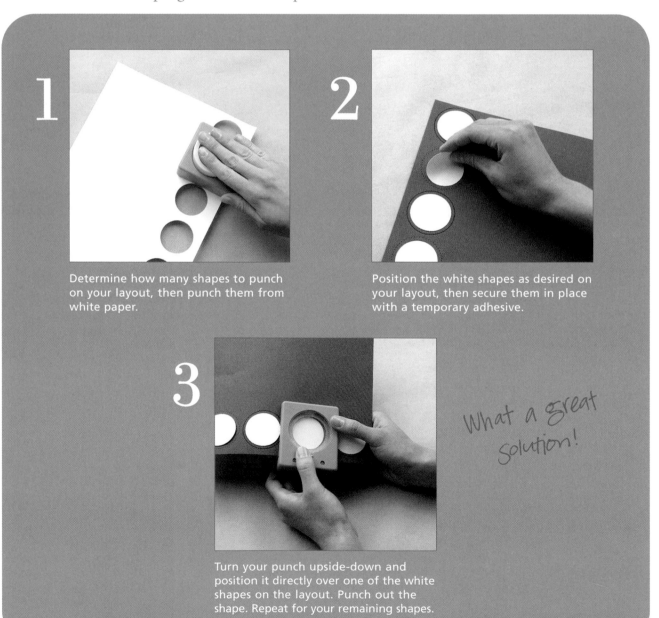

1 Determine how many shapes to punch on your layout, then punch them from white paper.

2 Position the white shapes as desired on your layout, then secure them in place with a temporary adhesive.

3 Turn your punch upside-down and position it directly over one of the white shapes on the layout. Punch out the shape. Repeat for your remaining shapes.

What a great solution!

bike rides

ERIN

TAKING IN THE SIGHTS. LAUGHING. TEASING. ENJOYING

MY FAVORITE SUMMERTIME ACTIVITY. ALWAYS AFTER DINNER. MATT AT MY SIDE. RIDING THROUGH THE NEIGHBORHOOD.

JUST LIKE BEING A KID AGAIN. JUST LIKE BEING A KID AGAIN. JUST LIKE BEING A KID AGAIN.

Create guides to make sure several punched shapes align. *Page by Erin Lincoln.* **Supplies** *Textured cardstock:* Bazzill Basics Paper; *Patterned paper, woven letters, metal stencil letter and concho:* Scrapworks; *Acetate letter:* Heidi Swapp for Advantus; *Rub-ons:* Doodlebug Design and KI Memories; *Brad and ticket accent:* Making Memories; *Circle punch:* EK Success; *Computer font:* 2Peas Tasklist, downloaded from *www.twopeasinabucket.com*; *Other:* Pens, button and embroidery floss.

Idea to note: Erin placed patterned paper behind a large, clear button to create a coordinated accent.

Stitched Accents

Need a little something to add subtle interest? Use a punch to create a stitching pattern! Simply punch a shape from scratch paper, then position it on your layout. Use a paper piercer to poke holes at even intervals around the shape. Remove the punched shape from your design and stitch along the pierced pattern with embroidery floss.

Use a punched shape as a guide for stitching beautiful accents. *Page by Erin Lincoln.* **Supplies** *Patterned papers:* Déjà Views, The C-Thru Ruler Co.; *Rub-ons and chipboard letters:* Heidi Swapp for Advantus; *Flower punch:* EK Success; *Bracket stickers:* American Crafts; *Buttons:* 7gypsies; *Computer font:* 2Peas Tubby, downloaded from *www.twopeasinabucket.com; Other:* Embroidery floss.

I've got to try this!

Vanessa Hoy, Senior Editor, SIP

Three Twists from CK Editors

I was curious what would happen if CK editors tried my techniques, so I asked who'd like to give them a shot. Three editors volunteered—here are three cool uses they came up with!

1 Make stencils from punches.

Punch shapes from scratch paper to create stencils for painting. *Pages by Vanessa Hoy.* **Supplies** *Textured cardstock:* Bazzill Basics Paper and Prism Papers; *Dimensional paint:* Texture Magic, Delta Creative; *Letter stickers:* American Crafts; *Stamping ink:* Stewart Superior Corporation; *Flower and heart punches:* Emagination Crafts; *Pen:* PermaBall, Pilot.

Idea to note: Vanessa used two heart punches as decorative "paper clips" on her layout.

This effect would look great with alphabet punches!

I loved how Erin used her flower punch as a stitching guide, but my favorite punches are small, with elaborate designs. I chose to punch flowers from a piece of leftover cardstock to create a stencil for painting. I then spread dimensional paint over the template with a texture comb so the intricate designs would visually "pop" from the page.

vanessa's notes

Liesl Russell, Editorial Assistant

2 Arrange several punched shapes into creative designs.

Layer punched shapes to create new and dimensional designs. *Card by Liesl Russell.* **Supplies** *Textured cardstock:* Bazzill Basics Paper; *Rub-ons:* Chatterbox; *Heart punch:* Emagination Crafts; *Ribbon:* Li'l Davis Designs.

Send off a card like this.

I liked Erin's idea to turn a simple punched shape into something more, so I tried layering a few punches to create a new look. I punched three hearts from cardstock, then curled the edges with my fingers. I positioned the hearts overlapping each other (with the tips toward the center).

Voilà—I'd created quick accents to make my card fun and unique! Try the same thing with flower shapes, leaf shapes and more. You can snip out segments with scissors for a textured look. Chalk or paint the accents' edges if desired.

liesl's notes

Leslie Miller, Special Projects Editor

3 Create patterns from additional products in your stash.

I should try this with my acetate letters & metal-rimmed tags.

Use a die cut as a simple guide for stitching accents. *Mini album by Leslie Miller.* **Supplies** *Textured cardstock:* Bazzill Basics Paper; *Bookplate:* Making Memories; *Computer font:* CK Cursive, "The Best of Creative Lettering" CD Combo, *Creating Keepsakes; Other:* Die cut, thread and embroidery floss.

When I first saw Erin's idea for using a punch as a stitching template, I was immediately reminded of a giraffe die cut I've had tucked away. Although I haven't created a layout that coordinates with the giraffe's bright colors and corrugated texture, the shape was perfect for the cover of a mini album I was making as a baby announcement.

I loved how easy the die cut made it to stitch the perfect giraffe, and I can still use the die cut when I find the perfect place for it. This technique would work great with a number of the supplies in my stash! ♥

leslie's notes

Not Just Another Pretty

ACCENT

3 ways to embellish with intent

When I started scrapbooking, I used accents sparingly. I preferred to stick with photo corners and brads and focus on photos and journaling. That didn't last long once I started working at *Creating Keepsakes* magazine. I've seen so many fun supplies—everything from pretty patterned paper to jars of paper flowers—that I'm hooked! Picking and choosing accents has become a major "fun factor" when I scrapbook.

Still, I'm careful to embellish with intent. I choose accents that serve a purpose, that not only look nice but enhance the story I'm trying to tell on my page. You can use an accent as a symbol, design inspiration or way to present ephemera. Here are three ways to embellish with intent. by Vanessa Hoy

Supplies *Patterned paper, ribbon and epoxy accents:* KI Memories; *Metal flowers:* Maya Road; *Fiber and beads:* Artgirlz; *Flower punch:* EK Success; *Buttons:* Buttons Galore and Making Memories; *Fabric flowers:* Fancy Pants Designs.

Get Symbolic

An artist paints images on canvas to embody ideals and concepts, while a poet works with words and language. As a scrapbooker, you express your vision through scrapbooking supplies. Use accents to represent traits or emotions. For example, a flower accent can represent femininity as well as nature, fragility or innocence.

Or, take a cue from the suggested meaning behind certain colors. Choose yellow accents to represent joy or cheerfulness or green accents to represent harmony, nature or hope.

Almost Sisters *by Kayla Schwisow.* **Supplies** *Patterned papers:* KI Memories and EK Success; *Letter stickers:* Creative Imaginations; *Corner rounder:* Creative Memories; *Eyelets:* Wal-Mart; *Ribbon:* Making Memories; *Computer fonts:* Noodle Script, downloaded from the Internet; 2Peas Samantha, downloaded from *www.twopeasinabucket.com; Other:* Dimensional foam adhesive.

Note how Kayla used two pieces of patterned paper to represent two different personalities. She unified the two patterns with grosgrain ribbon and eyelets.

Draw from the Design

Do your photos contain a lot of movement? When scrapbooking them, duplicate the look by incorporating curves and accents with vibrant colors. Or select a subtle color in your photograph, such as the color of your subject's eyes, and let that inspire the color scheme and page elements.

While walking along the Seattle waterfront, I found myself drawn to the action at Pier 54. The expectation of food on demand was as obvious as the willingness of the patrons to satisfy it. I found this strangely symbiotic relationship fascinating and spent a huge amount of time entranced by the

GULLS at Ivar's

Gulls at Ivar's by Sue Thomas. **Supplies** Textured cardstock and washer: Bazzill Basics Paper; Die-cut machine: QuicKutz; Letter stickers: Vintage Alphabet, me & my BIG ideas; Brads and acrylic paint: Making Memories; Computer font: Zurich, downloaded from the Internet; Other: Ribbon.

Sue added a bosher (a button/washer accent) to represent a buoy. She placed it strategically to complete the orange visual triangle.

Rolling His Eyes *by Traci Turchin.*
Supplies *Vellum, letter stickers and pen: American Crafts; Acrylic paint: Making Memories.*

To play off this photo of her husband rolling his eyes at her, Traci included an abundance of circles—from the layout to the curved title and journaling.

Ephemera

Sometimes the perfect accent is something you already have on hand—it could even be the reason for your page. Consider tags from a favorite outfit, or fabric swatches from a special sewing project.

If you prefer not to include the original item (such as a report card or diary entry), scan and print a copy to create personalized patterned paper. Use memorabilia pockets or shaker boxes to display smaller memorabilia on your page without altering them.

CHOOSING YOUR NAME WAS CERTAINLY A LOT OF WORK! I LOOKED THROUGH SEVERAL BOOKS AND EVERY ONLINE BABY NAME SITE I COULD FIND. I ORIGINALLY INTENDED TO CALL YOU GRACE. IN FACT, UP UNTIL YOU WERE BORN, CONNOR REFUSED TO CALL YOU ANYTHING ELSE! BUT I STARTED TO CHANGE MY MIND WHEN I STARTED TO LOOK AT THE DIFFERENT NAMES OF CHILDREN ON LAYOUTS IN SOME OF MY FAVORITE SCRAPBOOKING MAGAZINES. I SWEAR EVERY NAME I LIKED WAS THAT TAKEN FROM A FLOWER; DAISY, ROSE, LILY AND VIOLET! PERHAPS IT'S BECAUSE YOUR DADDY DOESN'T SEND ME ENOUGH OF THEM ~ HINT, HINT ;) FINALLY, WE DECIDED ON LILLIAN GRACE. LILY FOR SHORT! WE JUST FELL IN LOVE WITH THE NAME LILLIAN WHEN WE HEARD IT; IT JUST HAS SUCH AN OLD FASHIONED CHARM. AND I GOT MY FLOWER NAME, TOO! I LOVE YOU, LILY!

08/04

Lily *by Jennifer Bourgeault.* **Supplies** *Textured cardstock:* Bazzill Basics Paper; *Circle punch:* Creative Memories; *Cutting template:* Coluzzle; *Bookplate:* KI Memories; *Rub-ons:* Autumn Leaves; *Computer font:* CopprplGoth BT, Microsoft Word; *Other:* Silk flowers from headband.

Jennifer wanted to preserve her daughter's headband, so she removed a few silk flowers and placed them on the page. They help her remember how tiny her daughter once was.

Most mothers receive dandelions and wild flowers from the tiny little fists of their children. But not me! For as long as you have been walking outdoors, YOU HAVE BEEN BRINGING ME ROCKS. When we walk along the roadside, you stop to pick up a rock. As we stroll along the lakeshore, you chase the tide to snatch a rock. When you're digging in the dirt piles, you are delighted to excavate a rock for me. "Look Mom! I found you a pretty rock!" Yes, I have quite a collection - rocks fill jars, act as paperweights, knick knacks and flower garden accents. They range in every color, shape and size. I am a pretty lucky mom, I love my rocks. And the greatest thing about your gifts, is that although flowers will wither and die, your rocks will remain a constant reminder of your boyhood days, and OUTSTRETCHED HANDS BRINGING ME ROCKS.

You Bring Me Rocks *by Rita Shimniok.* **Supplies** *Patterned papers:* Memories Complete and unknown (blue crackle); *Textured cardstock:* Bazzill Basics Paper; *Brads:* Making Memories; *Distressing ink:* Ranger Industries; *Twill:* Wright & Co.; *Dimensional glaze:* Plaid Enterprises; *Computer fonts:* Jester and Cherub, downloaded from the Internet; *Other:* Slide mount.

Rita embellished her slide mount with the tiny rocks her son gave her last summer.

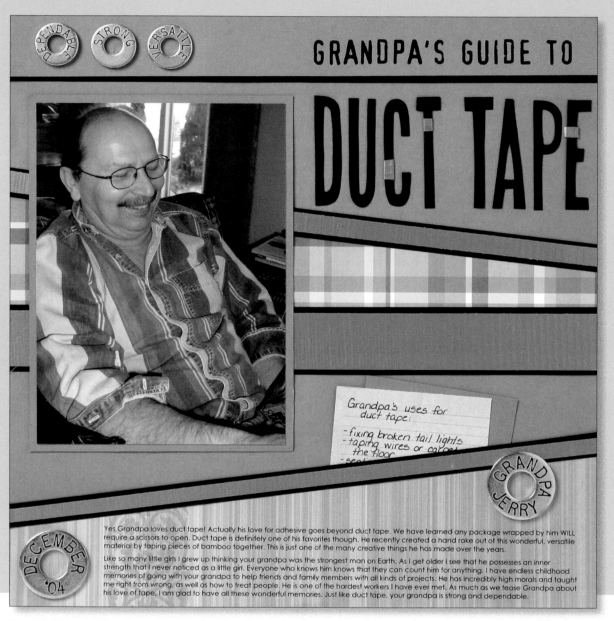

GRANDPA'S GUIDE TO

DUCT TAPE

DEPENDABLE · STRONG · VERSATILE

GRANDPA JERRY

DECEMBER '04

Grandpa's uses for duct tape:
- fixing broken tail lights
- taping wires or carpet the floor
- seal

Yes Grandpa loves duct tape! Actually his love for adhesive goes beyond duct tape. We have learned any package wrapped by him WILL require a scissors to open. Duct tape is definitely one of his favorites though. He recently created a hand rake out of this wonderful, versatile material by taping pieces of bamboo together. This is just one of the many creative things he has made over the years.

Like so many little girls I grew up thinking your grandpa was the strongest man on Earth. As I get older I see that he possesses an inner strength that I never noticed as a little girl. Everyone who knows him knows that they can count him for anything. I have endless childhood memories of going with your grandpa to help friends and family members with all kinds of projects. He has incredibly high morals and taught me right from wrong, as well as how to treat people. He is one of the hardest workers I have ever met. As much as we tease Grandpa about his love of tape, I am glad to have all these wonderful memories. Just like duct tape, your grandpa is strong and dependable.

Grandpa's Guide to Duct Tape by Lisa Dorsey. **Supplies** *Textured cardstock:* Bazzill Basics Paper; *Patterned papers:* Chatterbox and Creative Imaginations; *Letter rub-ons:* Autumn Leaves; *Computer fonts:* Hootie!, downloaded from the Internet; Century Gothic, Microsoft Word; *Other:* Duct tape and washers.

As a fun twist, Lisa actually included duct tape on her page! ♥

Flower Power

Let spring blossom on your pages

NOTHING SAYS SPRING like the debut of flowers—pale pink cherry blossoms, vivid tulips and happy daffodils never fail to put a spring in *my* step. Bringing the garden indoors and onto your scrapbook pages is easy and painless when you add a touch of handmade style to pre-made flower embellishments. Let me show you some of my ideas!

by Candice Stringham

flowers
on the fly

I wanted to create a whimsical look to complement a playful photo. First, I marked a pattern with a white chalk fabric pencil. After sewing along my marks, I attached the flowers with a simple French knot in the center of each. The stitched pattern almost looks like the wind carrying flower petals right alongside my little runner!

I'll Fly Away *by Candice Stringham.* **Supplies** *Textured cardstock: Bazzill Basics Paper; Flower accents: Prima; Other: Thread.*

To create a French knot:

1 Thread your needle and knot the end of the thread. Insert the needle through the back of your background paper or fabric and pull tight.

2 Wrap thread around your needle two times (more if you want a bigger knot).

3 Pull the needle back through near the original hole. Avoid pulling it through the original hole or you'll undo your stitch!

pretty petals

I used Prima flowers to create this monogram. The look takes a little time, but the results are well worth it. Follow these simple steps to get the same look.

1 Print a monogram in your chosen font. Glue the letter to a piece of chipboard and cut out the letter.

2 Using small, fine-tipped scissors, carefully cut the petals from the flowers.

3 Coat the monogram with glue and let it get a little tacky. *Note:* I used a small paintbrush and a glue called PVA. This bookbinding glue can be found online, but any craft glue that doesn't dry too quickly will work.

4 Beginning at the bottom, place the petals in rows, slightly overlapping each to cover the background.

5 Repeat until you reach the top. Wrap the tip of the petal over the top to cover the chipboard.

Miss You *by Candice Stringham.* **Supplies** *Patterned papers:* Scenic Route Paper Co., Chatterbox and Wild Asparagus, My Mind's Eye; *Flower accents:* Prima; *Other:* Silk leaves and CD tin.

Variations:

❀ Use a variety of colored petals to create a pattern.

❀ Don't forget the leaves! They also make beautiful monograms when repeated.

flower
fusion

"He loves me, he loves me not." You know the game—every pre-teen girl has played it at least once, plucking one petal at a time until the last one falls with either the thrilling "he loves me" or the devastating "he loves me not." My husband is really good to me, so I created a

layout celebrating the reasons I love my husband.

I backed each flower with book cloth, and instead of using a traditional brad, I challenged myself to find unique ways to attach each flower. See if you can think of more!

How Do I Love Thee? *by Candice Stringham.* **Supplies** *Textured cardstock:* Bazzill Basics Paper; *Bookplate, brads and tag:* Making Memories; *Metal frame:* Pebbles Inc.; *Page pebble:* K&Company; *Letter tile:* Jo-Ann Scrap Essentials; *Computer font:* Laine Day, downloaded from the Internet; *Other:* Silk flowers, book cloth, raw silk (red), felt, embroidery thread and rub-ons.

To get the same look for each of these
flower creations:

After arranging three small silk flowers, attach them using a simple cross-stitch in the center of each flower. Clip a few leaves from a bouquet of silk flowers and use rub-ons for the lettering. *Note:* I found these flowers at a basic craft store. I even used the leaves from a different bouquet of flowers, so mixing and matching is fine!

Cut an original flower design from felt and blanket-stitch the flower to your background. Sew a black seed bead to each stitch for added texture. Finish off the look with a black button center. *Note:* To avoid mistakes when cutting the flower, make a template from paper or thick cardstock.

To create a blanket stitch:

1 Insert a threaded sewing needle through the backside of the flower, ¼" from the edge. Pull thread tight.

2 Place the flower on the background paper or fabric and insert the needle through the background and the flower ¼" away from the edge. Pull the thread tight.

3 Insert the needle up through the background (off the edge of the flower) ¼" above the second stitch.

4 Place the needle under the original stitch and pull it to the edge.

5 Repeat steps 1–4 around the entire border of the flower.

6 To finish the stitch, catch the first stitch with your needle so it forms a square.

I liked the idea of a botanical garden, where they label each flower with a nameplate beneath each bloom, as inspiration for this look. Place a bookplate across a simple paper flower and use green snaps to hold it in place.

Looks like a lot of work, doesn't it? This is actually a pre-made flower sticker. You can make your own by adding sequins and doing another blanket stitch with seed beads.

I loved this flower but it was too big for the page. The solution? I cut the flower in half, removed unwanted petals, then stapled it back together, creating the perfect size. Finishing this flower off with a photo center made it a perfect focal point for this page.

To get this look, use a brad with a loop. Attach the picture frame with waxed linen thread. *Note:* Thread is most often used to sew pages together during the bookbinding process and can be found online at bookbinding sites. It is strong, safe for scrapbooking, and available in a multitude of colors.

Dress up a flower with a piece of eye-catching ribbon and a square knot.

Cover a printed title with a clear page pebble to create the center of a flower. It's an easy way to customize your title.

Place a word tile over your flower to add a personal touch. ♥

Timeless Ribbon

30 quick and easy ribbon ideas

My ribbon stash makes me feel cheerful and happy. It's like my own little garden of colorful flowers in bloom all year round! I love it all: the crisp grosgrain, the charming vintage prints, the sophisticated stripes and the ruffled romantic strands.

Ribbon is more than just eye candy for scrapbookers, however. It's also a great design tool that can take a layout from basic to brilliant in just minutes. I challenged myself and three designers to create layouts using just cardstock, a pen and ribbon. Take a peek at our results, then challenge yourself to do the same!

by Shelley Laming

Fill a Shape

At first glance, this diamond border appears to have been created with patterned paper—right? Instead, Mellette filled the shapes with angled ribbon strips, giving the layout texture and dimension. I love the flower she made by fringing three cardstock circles and securing the layers together with a knot of ribbon in the center. And don't forget how much possibility a simple pen can hold. Mellette added original hand-drawn designs that rival any stamp or rub-on! Note how the simple ribbon loops at the top of the page draw attention to the title.

Girlfriends *by Mellette Berezoski.* **Supplies** *Cardstock:* Making Memories, Bazzill Basics Paper and WorldWin; *Ribbon:* Making Memories, May Arts, KI Memories, Strano Designs and Michaels; *Pen:* American Crafts.

Or try . . .

- The same fill technique with other shapes.
- Creating the outline of a shape using ribbon or trim.
- Giving the diamonds more punch by outlining them with black pen.
- Replacing the row of diamonds with a row of colorful fringed cardstock flowers with ribbon centers.

Mix Textures

I love mixing textures on my pages and often rely on ribbon to do the job. Here I mixed a wide contemporary striped ribbon with printed twill, grosgrain, vintage flocked trim and an intricate rosebud ribbon—an easy border technique that anyone can pull off! To draw the eye away from the seatbelt strap showing in the bottom of the photo, I overlapped two pieces of ribbon on the photo and pulled them through it.

Sweet Face *by Shelley Laming.* **Supplies** *Ribbon:* May Arts, Strano Designs, 7gypsies and The Lion Company; *Pen:* Zig Writer, EK Success; *Other:* Rosebud ribbon.

Or try . . .

- Creating borders around a photo or the perimeter of the page.
- Adding details to the ribbon strips with bow ties, charms or accents.
- Using ribbon to write the title.
- Placing ribbon right on a photo to cover up little blunders.
- Creating an original patterned-paper look by filling the entire left-hand side of the page with ribbon strips.

Combine Colors and Patterns

I often reach for ribbon to add a soft, home-spun touch, so I love that Lisa showed me how to put a bold, graphic twist on ribbon in this layout. Using a simple weave technique, she combined ribbons of varying colors and patterns while effectively framing her photo with a photo corner in the upper-right-hand corner. Lisa created visual interest with different widths and lengths of ribbon.

Genuine Boy *by Lisa McGarvey.* **Supplies** *Textured cardstock:* Bazzill Basics Paper; *Pens:* Slick Writers (black), American Crafts; Uni-ball Signo (white), Sanford; *Ribbon:* KI Memories, C.M. Offray & Son, Creative Imaginations and Strano Designs.

Many people balk at the thought of using their own handwriting, but it's a quick and easy way to record information and add a unique decorative touch.

Or try . . .

- Using ribbon to create photo corners around all four (or just a couple) corners of your photo.
- Using solid ribbon for a different look.

Fashion Some Fancy Flaps

I made handwritten text the star of this layout. To create the decorative ribbon flaps at right, I cut five vertical slits and threaded one end of the ribbon from beneath the page and through each slit. I secured the other end to the page with staples. You can alter this simple technique as much as your heart desires!

Shelley's 5 never-ever-fail bad day busters:

1. tight hugs from Ned.
2. pick a fresh bouquet of flowers.
3. laugh with the girls... belly laughs are good for the soul.
4. ..trail after a butterfly...
5. remind myself there's always someone who has it worse!

Bad Day Busters by Shelley Laming. **Supplies** Pen: Zig Writer, EK Success; Ribbon: Doodlebug Design, May Arts and C.M. Offray & Son; Punches: EK Success; Other: Staples.

Or try . . .

- Placing ribbon tabs around photos or the edges of the page.
- Using ribbon for bullet points or arrows to draw attention to each item on a list.
- Making a grid with ribbon and writing each journaling item inside one of the weaved blocks.

Try Funky Touches

Jennifer created flower petals by looping ribbon strands, arranging them in a circle and adding a cardstock circle to the center. She gave the flowers a whimsical look by doodling on the cardstock centers.

Summer Is . . . *by Jennifer Johner.* **Supplies** *Ribbon:* Rhonna Farrer for Autumn Leaves and Making Memories; *Pen:* Zig Millennium, EK Success; *Computer font:* Gilligan's Island, downloaded from the Internet.

For more great techniques, along with cool ribbon ideas from Erin Lincoln, visit us online at www.creatingkeepsakes.com.

Or try . . .

- Using printed twill or pieces of ribbon to get the same mosaic look around your photo.
- Altering the flowers with cardstock petals and ribbon centers.

Make a Motif

Ribbon doesn't have to simply accent—it can easily become one of the focal decorative elements of the page. I placed various ribbons at a diagonal angle to create this ribbon motif, mixing print and script for added variety. I used my black pen to accent different strips of ribbon by outlining some of them once or twice.

Cassidy and Chandler *by Shelley Laming.* **Supplies** *Pen:* Zig Writer, EK Success; *Ribbon:* Kate's Paperie (pom-pom ribbon), Making Memories and C.M. Offray & Son.

Or try . . .

- Tucking items, such as extra journaling, booth photos, memorabilia and more, behind the ribbons.
- Creating a vertical ribbon pattern.

- Hanging simple cardstock tags at varying heights from the diagonal ribbons. Each tag could have a small snippet of journaling, a simple icon or a one-liner that's an inside joke between friends. ♥

i think i was saved,
because she let me ramble in her ear,
and i found strength in her reason,
oh i found myself in her, dear... *Brenda Weiler

exquisite embroidery

THIS YEAR'S NATIONAL STATIONERY SHOW included several irresistible looks. One of the hottest? Embroidered designs! The next time you'd like to add an artistic touch to a creation, consider a simple embroidered accent. Or, kick things up a notch by stitching a sequin, bead or rhinestone to your design. You'll love the look! ♥

Embroider on small scraps of cardstock or fabric—or directly on your page. *Page by Nisa Fiin.* **Supplies** *Cardstock:* Bazzill Basics Paper; *Patterned papers:* American Crafts and My Mind's Eye; *Letter stamps:* PSX Design; *Stamp:* Purple Onion; *Stamping ink:* Distress Ink, Ranger Industries; *Pen:* Sharpie, Sanford; *Adhesive:* Mono Adhesive, Tombow; *Circle punch:* Marvy Uchida; *Embroidery floss:* DMC.

Consider embroidery floss from the following companies:

❶ DMC
www.dmc-usa.com

❷ Janlynn
www.janlynn.com

❸ Kreinik
www.kreinik.com

❹ Lasting Impressions for Paper
www.lastingimpressions.com

❺ Hot Off The Press
www.paperwishes.com

TRY THESE FIVE Sweet IDEAS

Every few weeks, my mother sets up shop in front of the TV. She pulls out her ironing board and a can of spray starch, then irons for hours until her pile of clothes turns into a long line of perfectly pressed garments.

With the example set by my domestic diva mother, you'd think I could iron. Truth be told, my husband does it all. If I need a skirt ironed, I ask him. Me, press those work pants? Don't make me giggle. I wouldn't know where to start. My mother even laughed out loud when I told her I was writing an article involving an iron.

Actually, if ironing were as fun with clothes as it is with scrapbooking, I might not have turned out so clueless about laundry. Still, when I saw some iron-on embellishments, I decided to pull out my iron. I was even able to create some fun designs and techniques for my pages. Let me share what I came up with!

BY ERIN LINCOLN

WHAT'S AN IRON-ON?

An iron-on transfer is a mirror image of a graphic or text that's transferred to your project with the heat from an iron. The heat melts the adhesive in the iron-on, adhering and sealing it to your desired surface.

Iron-ons come in assorted colors, finishes and designs, and you can use them to create shiny, sparkling, raised or flocked textures for your pages. While you'll find different types (some are designed specifically for fabric while others are designed specifically for paper), the two are interchangeable for all your needs.

GETTING STARTED

TO CREATE A PROJECT WITH IRON-ONS, YOU WILL NEED:

* An iron, set on the "cotton" (no steam) setting
* A heat-resistant surface, such as an ironing board
* Iron-on embellishments
* Directions. Pay close attention since they vary by brand, each having different requirements. For the best results, follow the step-by-step directions provided by the manufacturer.

IN GENERAL, FOLLOW THESE STEPS:

1. Heat your iron.
2. Cut your desired design out of the surrounding images (often, multiple iron-ons come on a single sheet), leaving the backing intact.
3. Place the design face-down on your layout, with the backing face-up.
4. Press the iron on top of your design and move it continuously over the area for 10–15 seconds. Remove.
5. Let the design cool down for a few seconds. Tease up the edge of the backing with your fingernail. If the design transferred, it will remain on the project surface; peel the rest of the backing away.

If the design didn't transfer, it will remain on the backing sheet (you'll notice this when you start to peel the backing). Reapply heat with the iron and repeat until the design peels away from the backing.

FUN TWISTS

After getting used to the basic directions of using iron-ons, I created some neat variations. Check out these examples.

Three hours to pull together a last minute birthday party for Mom which was to include homemade dinner and cake, presents, and themed decorations? Bring it on. Elizabeth, Matt, and I rushed around like mad hatters one Friday afternoon and pulled it off. It was just a coincidence that all of us girls just happened to be wearing pink that day...made the pink princess theme (snort!) a snap to pull off. Dinner was a fabulous BBQ kabob feast thanks to Matt, devoured by all. And notice the double tier plate of chocolate cupcakes? Mom said she got two wishes out of that arrangement. As for Dad...we taught him how to suck the helium out of the balloons to make his voice go all squeaky. He changed Mom's voice mail message while under the influence. He, and everybody else, had a ball. Happy 53rd Birthday Mom! We love you so much.

fabulous
sister mom party

Fabulous *by Erin Lincoln.* **Supplies** *Textured cardstock:* Prism Papers; *Patterned papers:* BasicGrey, Scrapworks and KI Memories; *Vellum and pen:* American Crafts; *Stickers:* SEI and American Crafts; *Rub-ons and stamps:* FontWerks; *Concho and sticker:* Scrapworks; *Stamping ink:* Stampin' Up!; *Iron-ons:* Heidi Swapp for Advantus; *Computer font:* Times New Roman, Microsoft Word.

Iron the first three letters on to vellum and cut out the shapes.

Experiment with TEXTURES

Iron your embellishments onto textured surfaces, such as vellum and suede paper, for extra impact. In "He Loves Me Anyway," I layered the iron-ons over suede paper—I love the feel of the combinations.

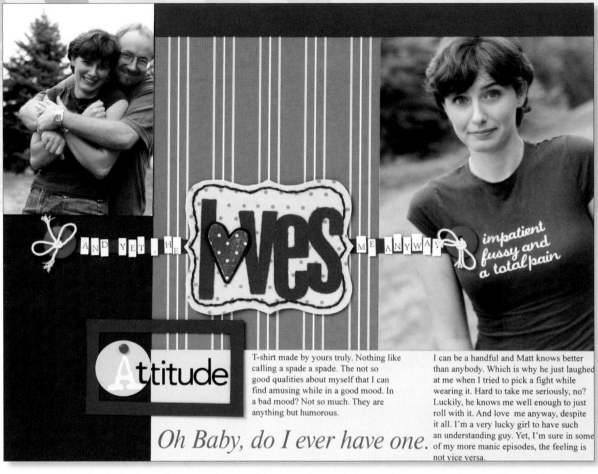

He Loves Me Anyway by Erin Lincoln. **Supplies** *Patterned papers:* Wild Asparagus by My Mind's Eye; *Velvet paper:* SEI; *Rub-ons, metal tag and letter stickers:* Making Memories; *Buttons and brads:* American Crafts; *Iron-ons:* Heidi Swapp for Advantus; *Punch:* EK Success; *Computer font:* Times New Roman, Microsoft Word.

HAVE A LITTLE FUN

I admit it. I used some of my iron-ons to create a fun T-shirt. (Hey, the idea of using iron-on embellishments for scrapbook pages was borrowed from clothing design.)

Why not take the idea full circle and design yourself a fun T-shirt for a photo shoot? You can wear it later to the gym or to bed. (No, I'm not crazy enough to wear this one out in public!)

LAYER Your Iron-On Elements

To create this layout, I first ironed the snowflake (it has a raised, flocked design) onto my page. Next, I ironed my title letters over the snowflake.

Since the snowflake was raised, the letters melted down into all the crevices, resulting in a wrinkled design. The cool results were a total fluke, but I love it when that happens!

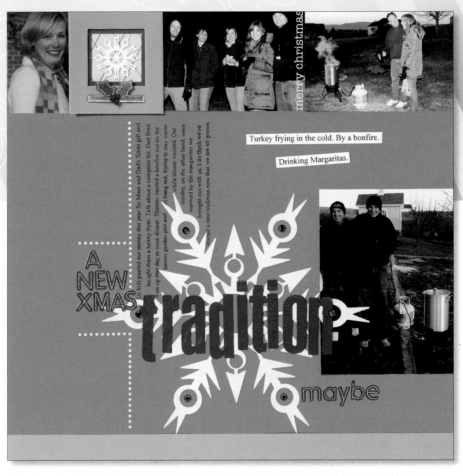

A New Xmas Tradition by Erin Lincoln. **Supplies** *Patterned paper:* Treehouse Designs; *Stickers and brad bar:* Karen Foster Design; *Rub-ons:* Making Memories and KI Memories; *Iron-ons:* SEI and Heidi Swapp; *Chipboard frame:* Heidi Swapp for Advantus; *Computer font:* Times New Roman, Microsoft Word; *Other:* Mini rhinestones.

Devoted solely to alphabets, Heidi Swapp iron-ons can add a fun and colorful touch to your pages. Select from uppercase and lowercase styles in three fonts: Apple pie, Newsprint and Center of Attention. The iron-ons are available in six colors (betty, crimson, jet, pink, sea and white), with "fuzzy" and glitter styles to match the mood of your layout.

Heidi Swapp
MSRP: $8.99
Web site:
www.heidiswapp.com

Just promise me you'll treat her like a princess.

A New Boyfriend
Brian and Elizabeth

A New Boyfriend *by Erin Lincoln.* **Supplies** *Patterned papers, button and pen:* American Crafts; *Chipboard letters:* Making Memories; *Iron-ons:* SEI; *Computer font:* Times New Roman, Microsoft Word.

Add a splash of color!

COMBINE with Cardstock

When I saw these great iron-ons with an open flower and leaf design, I immediately thought they would look great with splashes of color in the negative spaces. I love how it turned out. Follow these steps to create a similar look with any type of open design, such as flowers, stars or open letters.

❶ Cut out design from iron-on sheet.

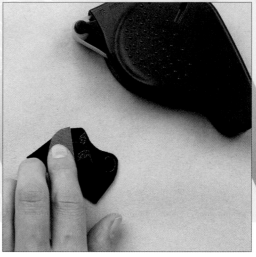

❷ Use temporary adhesive to secure a small scrap of colored cardstock over the open part of the design.

❸ Iron design onto project.

❹ Trim away the extra cardstock that's sticking out from the edges of your design. (Micro-tip scissors work best.) *Note:* The portion of the design with the colored cardstock piece behind it will not have adhered to the background paper. Adhere it in place with a permanent adhesive.

Looking for a graphic image to add that extra touch to your page? You'll find a wide selection from SEI. Designs are classified into 11 categories (basics, velvet treasures, graphic wear, alphabet letters, numbers, harvest, seasons in the sun, snow days, bead-dazzle, vivid vibes and glitz) and offer multiple color schemes.

SEI
MSRP: $1.50–$4
Web site: *www.shopsei.com*

Boston *by Erin Lincoln.* **Supplies** *Album:* 7gypsies; *Chipboard letter stencils, tape, chipboard strips and shapes:* Heidi Swapp for Advantus; *Tag and tacks:* Chatterbox; *Ribbon alphabet, foam stamp and woven photo corner:* Making Memories; *Stamping ink:* Ranger Industries; *Sticker:* Karen Foster Design; *Iron-on transfer paper:* Avery.

Iron on Your PHOTOS

I found printable iron-on sheets at an office supply store, then printed mirror images of my photos onto them. I used the photos to personalize chipboard letter stencils for an album cover using the following steps:

1. Create a mirror image of your design, then print onto transfer paper.

2. Select white chipboard stencils or raw finished stencils painted white.

3. Trim your transfer to the same dimensions as your chipboard stencil.

4. Iron the transfer onto your chipboard. *Note:* Apply the heat for only as long as it takes the paper to adhere to the stencil—any longer will cause the design to become distorted.

5. Peel the backing away, leaving the design on the chipboard.

6. Use a craft knife to trim away the excess transfer image covering the negative space in the chipboard stencil.

7. Adhere the chipboard stencil to your project.

CREATE Your Own Designs

Kreinik makes iron-on thread in a variety of sizes and colors. You can use it to freehand your own designs or follow a pattern. On my "Friendship" accent, I looped the thread into flower petals and ironed it onto patterned paper. I covered the loose ends with a button (the button is covered with patterned paper). I cut out the flower, then attached it to the green background on my accent.

Friendship *by Erin Lincoln.* **Supplies** *Patterned papers:* Scrapworks and KI Memories; *Rub-ons:* KI Memories and Die Cuts With a View; *Rubber stamps:* FontWerks and Stampin' Up!; *Stamping ink:* ColorBox, Clearsnap; Ranger Industries; *Iron-on thread:* Kreinik; *Coverable button:* Prym-Dritz; *Pen:* American Crafts; *Other:* Alphabet beads.

Want to add dimension to your project but would rather create your own iron-on design? Check out the iron-on threads from Kreinik.

Available in braid (medium and fine) and ribbon styles, Kreinik offers over 30 thread colors. You'll also find 12 assortment packs that let you create one-of-a-kind designs, from flowers and waves to your own handwritten text. If you're creating intricate designs, you may want to invest in a small craft iron as well for extra control when you iron.

Kreinik
MSRP: $2.30 (spool), 6.95 (3-pack assortment)
Web site: *www.kreinik.com*

Drats! There's no hiding my newly acquired household skill. Six scrapbook projects tell the tale of my familiarity with the iron. My husband is relieved, my mother is proud, and I'm still in denial about it all. But I'm having fun! ♥

ask the experts

Q I love embellishments but find that using too many can take the focus away from the story I'm trying to tell. Is there a rule of thumb to decide what type or how many embellishments to include on a layout?

—JOYCE PARMLEY, TROY, OH

BECKY SAYS:

Becky Higgins • CK Contributing Editor

1 **great question, Joyce!** As scrapbookers we each form our own style and level of comfort for experimenting with products and techniques.

2 **if the embellishments** take attention away from your photographs, they're probably too much. Don't be afraid to use the coolest new products on the market. Just remember—moderation in all things. And keep a long-term perspective in mind. If you load your layout with a lot of new, trendy "stuff" (as opposed to including accents in a minimal way), you may cringe when you look at that layout in five years.

3 **if you feel** like you're forcing another cute embellishment on your page because you saw other people do it in the magazine, it's not really for you. Follow your instincts, and you'll retain the integrity of your style. ❯